A MURDER IN MY
HOMETOWN

New York Times Bestselling Author

Rebecca Morris

WILDBLUE
PRESS

WildBluePress.com

A MURDER IN MY HOMETOWN published by:

WILDBLUE PRESS
P.O. Box 102440
Denver, Colorado 80250

WILDBLUE PRESS is registered at the U.S. Patent and Trademark Offices.

ISBN 978-1-947290-67-9   Trade Paperback
ISBN 978-1-947290-66-2   eBook

Interior Formatting by Elijah Toten
www.totencreative.com

A MURDER IN MY
HOMETOWN

Table of Contents

DEDICATION

To the Corvallis High School Class of 1968

"The town, though attractive, was much of sameness. It had grown in a semicircle around a bend in the Sacajawea and now extended thinly to the western and northern hills, surrounding the long rectangle of green campus and red-brick college buildings."

— *A New Life, 1961, by Bernard Malamud*

"There are some places that the road doesn't go in a circle. There are some places where the road keeps going."

— *Pleasantville, 1998 film, by Gary Ross*

FALL 1967

THE MAYOR OF SEATON'S

Ten days in one of America's most polluted rivers had not been kind to the body. The cold water had slowed decomposition, but the nibbling of fish had made inroads. The body was bloated, filthy, and foul smelling, as contaminated as the water, sewage, and tree limbs that kept it hidden and submerged until it moved free of a branch or the body's gases caused it to float to the surface. On the afternoon of Saturday, October 21, 1967, thirteen-year-old Dan Eckles and his fourteen-year-old cousin, Jim Crawford, were fishing on the dock of Riverview Marina, the business Dan's dad had bought when he moved his family up from California. Dan and his three older sisters and parents lived in an apartment in the marina, which sat on the west bank of the Willamette River as it wound through Corvallis, Oregon. The longest river in North America traveling south to north – essentially uphill – was Dan's front yard. Some locals grumble and are quick to point out that no rivers *really* flow "uphill." But the river winds 200 miles through forest, farmland, and cities, growing from a mountain stream to a big river before joining the mighty Columbia. Dan and Jim fished mostly to waste time. The boys caught white fish and carp off the dock, but knew better then to keep what they caught. Just once Dan's family had fried up some fish from the river. They all got sick.

As they fished, Dan spotted something in the water. "It's not unusual to see something float by," he said later. But this was a body. "It was face down. It was about a foot and a half from me. I remember I started to reach out to it." He began to grab one of the body's arms but an irrational thought stopped him. What if it came off? He ran for his father, a former Los Angeles sheriff's detective. It would be awhile before Dan fished again.

Detective Sergeant Jim Montgomery was at the river when the body was pulled ashore and photographed. "It was ugly, black, there was green moss on him, there was a chain around his mouth," he said. The police had a long-standing joke about bodies found in the river. "Tow him over there," they'd say, pointing to the east side of the river. Then it would be the purview of Linn County.

But this one was theirs. The body was taken by hearse to McHenry Funeral Home on NW 5th. By the time it arrived, police suspected it could be that of a teenager who had been missing for ten days, seventeen-year-old Dick Kitchel. His father and stepmother had initially shrugged off his disappearance. They weren't worried. Maybe he was off at the coast with friends. They had finally gone to the police after Dick didn't show up for school one Monday. The police department considered him a runaway.

Ralph and Sylvia Kitchel met Montgomery, Captain Bill Hockema, and Assistant Police Chief Ken Burright at the funeral home. District Attorney Frank Knight; the coroner, Dr. Peter Rozendal; and the state medical examiner, Dr. Russell Henry, were also in attendance. Autopsies were routinely conducted at funeral homes. At McHenry, they shared space with a room on the main floor where embalming was performed. It was efficient. Showing little emotion, Ralph identified the body. It was Dick, a sweet boy as a child. He'd outgrown Cub Scouts and had become one of the tough guys, a teenager known for his beer drinking, a drunken car crash and arrest just weeks before his disappearance, and fist fights. Lots of fights, including ones with his dad. One of the first officers called to the river, Lieutenant Roger Schmeltz, had been to the Kitchel home to break up fights between father and son. But Dick was well-liked and had friends in every stratum of high school life. Although one friend described him as "always striving to be better than where he came from," at some point he seemed to have given up on the goal. His childhood had not been easy. He was an only child and his mother, Joan, had moved back to Washington state after her divorce. Both of his parents had remarried; his father for the third time just a few months before Dick's disappearance. Dick bounced between living and attending school in Olympia and being sent back to Corvallis. He lived to get out of the house, according to a friend.

The body had no identification or wallet. But it was Dick. He was dressed in jeans and a gray Oregon State University t-shirt. He also wore a JC Penney undershirt, JC Penney briefs, and a pair of white crew socks with black and olive stripes. The only items in his pockets were two nickels, two pennies, a brass key, and a white handkerchief. Dick had died with his beloved Acme cowboy boots on. Ralph had his own shoe repair business but his first shop in Corvallis was in the back of an Acme store. In a murder case, clothing is held onto indefinitely. But they asked Dick's father if he would eventually want the clothes and boots returned. He said no.

Dick owned two other items that meant the world to him. One was his baby blue '55 Chevy. The other was his Pacific Trail tan suede jacket. He never went anywhere without the car and the coat. The car was history – at least until Dick found the money for repairs. He had cracked it up over Labor Day weekend in a spectacular accident, taking out a row of mailboxes and trees and 150 feet of cedar fence. He was arrested for drinking while driving, attempting to leave the scene, and resisting arrest. Where was his jacket? one of his parents asked. It was the kind of jacket that looked better the more it was worn, and Dick wore it a lot. Not on the hottest Indian summer days in the fall, but there weren't a lot of those in Oregon.

After Ralph Kitchel looked at the body and said, "Yes, that's my son," he and Sylvia quickly left the room. The coroner and the medical examiner undressed Dick. He was small, only five feet two inches tall, 125 pounds. It hadn't mattered when he played on the town's Parks & Recreation summer baseball team known as The Crocs, short for Crocodiles, in grade school. Everyone was small then. His light brown hair fell forward and swept to the right of his hazel eyes. They were shut now. While his friends had grown in height, Dick's persistent small size caused some teasing and helped him form a hard shell. But despite his recent journey into fights and drinking, he was popular and his many friends still called him by his childhood name, Dickie. He was dating at least two girls, one a cheerleader. Now his life was over. No more speeding in his car, spending time with girls, or drinking at private parties. No more evenings at Seaton's, the most popular hamburger hangout for Corvallis teenagers who wanted to see and be seen. He was known as "the Mayor of Seaton's" because of his frequent visits, notoriety, and reputation for both starting fights and breaking up fights between others.

According to his father, he was left-handed. There'd been a pretty good fight, presumably leading to his death. The knuckles on both hands were bruised and he may have struck someone in the mouth as he fought for his life. He had been hit in both eyes, which were bruised. He had also been hit in the nose and he had bled from his ears and his mouth. There was a three-inch wide bruise on his throat. His larynx had been crushed, causing him to suffocate. Rozendal and Henry concluded Dick had been strangled, but not with bare hands. Someone had used an arm or the sleeve of a coat. There was no water in his lungs or stomach, so he was dead before he entered the river. Even his blood, an essential part of its seventeen-year-old host, was ruined and couldn't tell investigators much. The body had been contaminated through and through by the river and any blood samples were putrid. The coroner may have tried to draw blood from Dick's heart. It can be a source of last resort, unless it, too, is decomposed.

At the funeral home, Montgomery and Hockema learned Dick had been to a party the night he disappeared. With information from Ralph and Sylvia Kitchel, they began to compile a list of names of Dick's friends. One of them, or a family member, had most likely murdered the mayor of Seaton's.

THE TOWN

This is a story about a hometown. Mine. It is a murder mystery and a mystery about memory.

Everyone who settled in the West came from somewhere else. My grandparents came to Oregon from Illinois and Iowa in the late 19th century, but family on both sides had been in America for hundreds of years. Corvallis was my mother's hometown for more than 90 years. One day when she was 97, living in Seattle near my brother and me and beginning to fade, she said, "I think I'll move back to Corvallis." I said I would go too. I knew she was daydreaming. She was homesick for a town that may not have really existed. Corvallis was our Brigadoon, a village unaffected by time, too good to be true and a gift to only the few. It didn't appear out of the mist to everyone.

While working on this story, I discovered that *my* Corvallis wasn't necessarily the Corvallis that my high school classmates grew up in. More than a few told me they couldn't wait to leave town. I knew I remembered it as more idyllic than it could possibly have been. Perhaps in response to my own life troubles, I saw the life my parents had and gave to my brother and me as the happiest time in my life and the only years that have been carefree.

My memories start in the 1950s. Each decade has its fears, and when I was a child, we were at war in Korea, worried about communist influences in America, and fearful of the Cold War and the arms race. In my third grade class at Roosevelt School, and in third grade classrooms all over Corvallis, we were taught cursive writing, Oregon history, and how to "duck and cover." We thought the danger was outside our town, maybe in Russia. But Corvallis had its secrets.

Third grade, and the study of Oregon history, came in 1959 for me. It was a huge year because it was the centennial of Oregon's statehood. There were parades and beard growing contests. It was a great year to be immersed in our state's history, but in our studies we never learned about the state's dirty secret, what a historian calls our "schizophrenic relationship with race." To this day, Oregon is home to the whitest city in the US, Portland, according to the 2010 census. It all began on the Oregon Trail.

Many pioneers came West to escape the conflict between the North and South. Settlers from the South and states bordering the South brought more than family antiques in their covered wagons. They brought their prejudices with them. Some brought slaves. Oregon, essentially, was "a Southern state transplanted to the North." During the Civil War, there was an underground movement to support the South and establish slavery in Oregon.

The draw for the pioneers who didn't veer off to the California goldfields or the ones east of the Cascades was the river and the rich farmland on both sides of it. It was a Garden of Eden. The Willamette Valley is 150 miles straight up and down the state of Oregon. The river named for it runs the entire length and then some. The river's basin forms the Willamette Valley, with the mountains of the Coast Range to the west and the Cascades to the east. Corvallis grew slowly, but by the time we were in high school, the population was about 35,000.

If the Oregon Territory, which included parts of what is now Washington, Idaho, Wyoming, and Montana, was going to truly be Southern in character, it needed laws. As early as 1844, the territory passed a series of measures designed to ban Negroes from settling in the area. When Oregon earned statehood, it prohibited slavery but also banned Negroes from living in in the state.

Some of the slaves who gained their freedom remained in Corvallis with the families who had owned them, and were even buried alongside their owners. People of color were prohibited from owning property, yet a few did, including a mother and daughter, former slaves, who bought up land in what became downtown Corvallis. When Eliza Gorman died in 1869, her obituary said she had "won the respect and confidence of the entire community," and a "large number of citizens" attended her funeral.

The first wave of the Ku Klux Klan came and went just after the Civil War, then died out. But by the 1920s, the KKK was flourishing again, including in Portland and Oregon's small towns. The KKK actively recruited members and had a presence on the University of Oregon campus in Eugene, and at what was then Oregon Agricultural College in Corvallis.

On September 30, 1922, some Kleagles, officers of the KKK charged with recruiting new members, hosted a dance in the Foster Building downtown on 2nd Street, later the Montgomery Ward building. On October 18, 1923, a story on the front page of *The Gazette-Times* reported that 300 Klansmen were expected to parade Corvallis streets. Because Corvallis was centrally located, it had been chosen as the site for a Klonvocation. Special trains brought Klansmen from all over the Willamette Valley to town. The next day, the newspaper reported that 500 Klansmen had assembled to take part in a Klonklave at a farm a mile north of Korvallis. Obviously the KKK liked to play with spelling and alliteration.

Led by a marching band, the Klansmen paraded through town in their "uniforms," a full-length white robe with a pointed hat and a piece of cloth covering the face except for the eyes. They made their way to a field "near Abe King's place" north of town, where there was an initiation complete with a flaming cross and speeches. Then they served sandwiches and coffee.

With no editorial comment, the *Gazette-Times* quoted a local KKK leader as stating, "The Klan stands for good in every form, for America, the perpetuation of American ideals, for 100 percent Americanism, and the finest men in the community are enrolled in its ranks." He went on to add: "The American woman has had as much to do with shaping the destiny of America as the American man. The Klan is attempting in every way to elevate the standard of women."

Like other towns across the West, racism was insidious. Corvallis' most exclusive place to bury the dead was Oaklawn Cemetery on Whiteside Drive. When it was laid out in 1935, the cemetery excluded people of color. The rules weren't changed until 1971.

By the 1950s and '60s, despite being a university community, our schools were still astonishingly white. The university didn't have an international faculty until decades later. There was less than a handful of black and Asian students in our high school. There was an uneasy racial, religious, and economic divide in Corvallis. Our parents were educated and we seemed to accept what minorities there were. But we were overwhelmingly white and Protestant. Just as slavery was left out of the curriculum, we may not have known that Corvallis had a history of being prejudiced against the "Oriental," Catholics, and Jews. Rocks were thrown through the windows of Catholic families in town. My classmate, Mark Goheen, whose family was just the fourth Jewish family to settle in Corvallis, remembers a seventh grade social studies teacher at Highland View Junior High locking eyes with him and telling the class that the Jews killed Jesus because he wasn't the messiah they were looking for. "I recall challenging him on that, and classmates congratulating me later for standing up to him," Mark said. "When I told my parents that he had also said 'I have nothing against Jews, some of my best friends are Jews,' they started laughing, which bewildered me because I had no context that this was a common anti-Semitic claim."

His parents, Harry and Molly Goheen, and their three children moved to Corvallis in the mid-1950s. Harry did not convert to Judaism, but the family followed Molly's faith and lived as a Jewish family. There was no temple in town, so they and other Jewish families met at the Unitarian Church. Goheen shook up things as much as anyone in Corvallis ever did. As a mathematician at the University of Chicago, and part of the Office of Naval Research, he had worked on the Manhattan Project, the research that led to development of the first nuclear weapons. But he became too progressive even for universities, refused to continue to work on germ warfare, and lost his teaching jobs at Syracuse, Iowa State, and University of Pennsylvania when he refused to sign loyalty oaths during McCarthyism. The FBI had a file on him, and tried to tell OSC it couldn't hire him, but the college did and he received tenure in 1959. As a professor of mathematics and computer science, Goheen was so dismayed by the lack of diversity in Corvallis that he started local branches of the NAACP and the ACLU. He led vigils and protests, spending his lunch hour often alone, standing in the rain, holding a sign protesting the Vietnam War.

The apple did not fall far from the tree. In the spring of 1966, the theme of the junior-senior prom was "Moonlight and Magnolias." The yearbook said the cafeteria, decorated as the entrance to an old Southern mansion, would long be remembered for its "beauty and splendor." When George Wallace, the pro-segregation governor of Alabama, heard of the prom, he wrote a letter to CHS student body president Rich Johnson saying how pleased he was that "you think of us and our Southern way of life." He recounted his own visit to Oregon to speak at the University of Oregon in 1964 and invited the people of Corvallis to visit Alabama. Rich gave the letter to the *Gazette-Times*, which printed it with a note from Rich that the letter had arrived during final exams and he hadn't had a chance to share it earlier. He asked readers to draw their own conclusions. Sixteen-year-old Mark Goheen replied to Wallace's letter with one of his own, also printed in the *G-T*: "As a student at Corvallis High School, I would like to extend my gratitude to the generous governor of Alabama, who wrote such a kind letter to us on behalf of the friendly people of his state. I am also pleased the governor wants me to come see him. I am glad I am the right color."

There had always been an uneasy racial and economic divide in Corvallis. Yet my classmates and I weren't racist – or was there a quiet racism? Maybe we hadn't been tested. The Pacific Northwest *was* tested after Pearl Harbor was bombed. As tens of thousands of Japanese Americans in Oregon and Washington were housed in internment camps, universities turned their back on their Japanese American students. At Willamette University in Salem, Oregon's capital, ten Japanese American students were forced to leave the school. At the University of Washington in Seattle, many "Jap Students," as they were called in a newspaper headline, were sent to colleges in Michigan, Minnesota, and Chicago that agreed to accept them. The government paid their way if they couldn't afford to leave. Teachers could be fired if they were married to a Japanese American. The prejudice at OSU was unfair, but less dramatic than some other schools: Japanese Americans were forbidden to use the university library after 8 p.m. It was open until 10 p.m.

To borrow Tolstoy's explanation about happy and unhappy families, towns are unhappy in their own way. Corvallis – with a classic town and gown environment if there ever was one –   smothered some people and set enormously high expectations for others. It made others feel excluded. My parents had friends from all walks of life. The father of my first boyfriend was a small business owner and was bitter about college people.

But from the beginning, the college was important to the town. It *was* the town. It began as Corvallis College in 1848, was renamed Oregon Agricultural College in 1897, became

Oregon State College in 1937, and renamed Oregon State University in 1961.

The town needed businesses like the one Dick's father ran, but there wasn't much intermingling socially except through us, their children. Ralph and Sylvia Kitchel drank and bowled at the Moose Lodge south of town. My parents would never have judged them, but their lives were different. At the dinner table, we talked about life, school, my father's work in radio, and church. Mark Goheen remembers that his family discussed politics, history, war, and racial injustice over meals.

I'm betting Dick's family didn't.

THE PARTYGOERS

It was late, a minute before midnight, but the element of surprise is important in a murder investigation. Detectives Montgomery and Hockema, with Assistant Chief Ken Burright, knocked on the door, and when it was answered, invited themselves in. Christmas had come early. Not only were Paul and Juddi Everts home, but Melvin "Mel" Plemmons and Doug Hamblin were visiting, exactly the young men they wanted to see. Their names had quickly made it to the top of a list of Dick's acquaintances — not necessarily friends, but people he partied with. This was the house and these were the people who may have been the last to see Dick. Like the last night of his life, the occupants of the house were engaged in a drinking game.

It had been a long day for the detectives. Montgomery was at the river when the body was pulled ashore. He, Hockema, and Burright had attended the autopsy and talked to Ralph and Sylvia Kitchel. Then they went to see Judy Appelman, who Ralph Kitchel identified as one of Dick's girlfriends. She lived at 1170 N. 17th Street, just a block north of the high school's football field. Montgomery and Hockema talked to Judy with her father, Duane Appelman, present. Judy was a junior in high school, one year younger than Dick. She had short hair, sometimes worn with a headband or a ribbon. She looked like the all-American teenage girl she was. She was a cheerleader all three years of high school, and an active member of the rally dance committee, the fire squad, and student council.

The detectives told her Dick's body had been found. But she already knew. It had been nearly twelve hours since he was spotted floating in the river and news traveled very fast in Corvallis, faster than the Willamette River. She first heard that Dick was missing, and later heard he had been found dead, from her older sister Molly, who was part of Dick's crowd at Seaton's.

"I didn't know what to say to the detectives," she said later, so she simply told them about her brief relationship with Dick. She had never had a boyfriend and her parents wouldn't allow her to date, but Dick was permitted to come to her house. Starting in the summer of 1967, they would sit on the dark pink velvet couch in the formal living room and talk while her parents sat in the family room and sipped cocktails. She was very shy. "We never held hands, we never kissed," she said. "I think he was impressed that I was a cheerleader." She was petite, and so was Dick, and she thought that was another reason he liked her. Since they were a year apart, she didn't have classes with Dick, but saw him at football and basketball games. She didn't remember him ever attending a rally dance.

Judy's parents were strict, so Judy and Molly snuck out to spend time at Seaton's. Custer's In-N-Out had rectangle-shaped burgers. A&W had root beer. Wagner's had cherry Cokes. The Big O had roller skating carhops. But only Seaton's Barbecue Pit had Gooey Burgers with a special sauce for 19 cents, as well as easy access to beer if you were looking for it. It was the place to be seen. "There was no indoor seating so you would get out of your car and get into the cars of others and smoke," Judy said. "The food didn't matter. You were there to 'tool the pit'" — in other words, to drive around aimlessly. Dick sometimes sat with her in Molly's car. She never saw Dick angry or drinking, and didn't think he had any enemies, but she knew he was a member of a "macho crowd that liked to fight."

On October 10, the night before Dick disappeared, Judy drove some girlfriends to Newport, due west on the Oregon coast, in the family's '54 Ford. It was Judy's sixteenth birthday and she had passed her driver's exam that day. The group attended a performance of The Patriots, a band made up of local Corvallis kids, including Dick's neighbor Bob Wadlow on guitar. Afterward, Judy sped back over US 20, a breathtakingly twisting, narrow road across the top of the Oregon Coast Range that dropped suddenly down into the Willamette Valley. She could usually tell before she entered the house if her father was asleep or not. Her parents enjoyed their cocktails every night, and her father's snoring could be heard from the driveway. Her parents often didn't know if their daughters were home or not.

Judy told the detectives what she knew about October 11, the day Dick disappeared. During the school day, she saw Dick in the parking lot behind the high school. Like Seaton's, it was a place to see and be seen, so much so that even if kids had skipped school, they would show up to check in with friends. It was the last time she saw Dick. She had heard Dick had gone to a card party, that there had been a fight, and that someone gave him a ride home. After the police talked to Judy, she phoned some friends and they came over. One of them suggested they go to Seaton's, so they did. Within a day or two, she heard the ominous announcement on the high school's public address system, news she already knew. Dick had been murdered. She read the details in the *Gazette-Times*.

It was 11:10 p.m. when the police officers left the Appelman home. They drove by the home of seventeen-year-old Mel Plemmons, at 717 W. Lewisburg Road. They believed Mel had been at the party the last night of Dick's life. No one was home. They sat in the car and took a moment to decide where to go next. At 11:59 p.m., they arrived at the home of Paul and Juddi Everts. The rental house at 521 N. 14th Street was a bungalow, two stories with three pillars framing a broad front porch. (Coincidentally, it was around the corner from the boarding house my grandmother ran forty years earlier.) There was a small backyard and a narrow driveway on one side of the home with a small detached garage all the way in the rear shared with the house next door. 521 N. 14th was smack in the middle of a neighborhood filled with college students in other rentals. Montgomery, Hockema, and Burright interrupted the party underway to break the news to the Everts, Doug Hamblin, and Mel Plemmons. The body of their friend, Dick Kitchel, last seen ten days before at that very house, had been found in the Willamette River. There was no reaction. No one gasped or cried out in surprise. It may not have been news to the people assembled. Like Judy, it seemed that they already knew Dick was dead. Had they heard gossip, or did they have first-hand knowledge?

Paul Everts was the son of an OSU chemistry professor. His brothers were an MD and a PhD, but his life was turning out differently. Paul, who had graduated from CHS in 1964, had married Juddi — born Judy Seavy, class of 1965 — in the spring of her senior year. Their daughter was born the same year. Paul worked as a surveyor's helper at Corvallis Sand and Gravel where Juddi worked in the office. The other semi-permanent member of the household was nineteen-year-old Pat Hockett, who also went by the name Pat Taylor, who was a live-in babysitter for the couple.

Dick knew the Everts because he was good friends with Juddi's younger sister, Dawn —born Donieta Seavy, CHS class of 1968. "His home life was not pleasant, neither was mine," Dawn said later. Their friendship was based on a shared angst and not romantic. "His dad drank a lot. My parents fought all the time. He didn't like going home." Dick could be outgoing and friendly but that night he was moody and spoiling for a fight. No one knew why. "He could get obnoxious, mouthy," she said.

Paul told the police that on October 11, Dick arrived drunk.

The guests at Everts' liked to play a game they called "pass out," which was exactly what it sounded like: how much could they drink before they passed out? There had been more than a dozen teenagers along with a few men in their twenties at the Everts' house the night of October 11. Most chipped in a few dollars to be able to drink. Why the Everts – with a young child and jobs – would host regular parties wasn't clear. Maybe the beer money added up and helped them make ends meet. Paul told the detectives there had been a disagreement and Dick had told Juddi to "get fucked." According to the detective's notes, Paul said he told Dick "that was just about enough of that kind of talk, and took him out onto the front porch of the residence and pushed him up against the banister of the porch and talked to him." Paul said he talked with Dick about "various problems which Kitchel was having and what he should do on two charges which were pending against him" in municipal court for drunk driving and resisting arrest. It sounded pretty fatherly, and not entirely true, to the detectives. Paul explained he had offered Dick an olive branch: if Dick would go back into the house and apologize to Juddi, all would be forgiven. Dick and Paul returned to the house and Dick apologized. Later, Paul would change his story and say the fight was between Doug and Dick. Others at the party said Dick never reentered the house.

Doug Hamblin told the police he was twenty-one, but he was twenty-three years old, divorced, and the father of a two-year-old girl. He had attended CHS off and on, but may or may not have graduated. Doug had a troubled history. He was close to his mother, Flo, who was married a total of eight times in her life – two men she married twice. As one family member said, she didn't smoke or drink – she married. Just like Flo looked at marriage as a new beginning, Doug bounced from odd job to odd job: selling car parts to drag racers, buying and selling airplane engines, and driving trucks cross-country. Sometimes he worked as a hunting and fishing guide with a brother. He had been angry his entire life, ever since a piece of a broken beer glass pierced his face and cost him the sight in his right eye when he was a child. According to one of his several wives, he lied and was mean and abusive, even after he quit drinking.

The detectives would learn that Doug had been at the Everts' house twice the night of October 11. Exactly why he was there so often, including when the detectives visited on October 21 and other times, is unclear. He told his part of the story to the detectives. On the night of October 11, some of the teenagers at the party wanted to leave and he offered to drive them home. It was just before midnight because Juddi remembered the television was on and *The Tonight Show Starring Johnny Carson* was underway. Marty, Mel, and Dick piled into Doug's fifteen-year-old, two-toned DeSoto four-door sedan. Because Marty had a midnight curfew, Doug first drove west to the Tucker house - 2055 Kings Road. Then he turned east on Circle Drive and north on Highland Way and headed to the Plemmons home at 717 W. Lewisburg Road.

Doug said that when he returned to town, Dick, who had been in the backseat, was sitting in the right front seat. But Dick refused to tell Doug where he lived. He told him to keep driving, that he didn't want to go home. Finally, Doug pulled over at 4th and B Street, near the state employment office, and helped Dick out of the car. The right front door, on the passenger side, was broken, and Doug told the detectives he stepped out of the car and stood in the street to have Dick exit the driver's side of the vehicle. Dick didn't want to get out and Doug said he pulled him out of the car. The last time he saw Dick, he was walking south. He then drove back to the Everts' house, arriving at 1:30 a.m., about 90 minutes after leaving. The detectives didn't ask why it had taken so long to drive a few miles, dropping two boys at their homes and one downtown. They asked to look at his hands. They checked his knuckles first; there were no recent bruises or scratches visible, and there were no marks around his face or mouth. But it had been ten days since Dick fought off *someone,* and Doug used his hands in his job as a sheet metal worker. The grease and grit imbedded in his hands could have masked any bruises or cuts. Doug was asked if he would take a lie detector test and he said he would, as long as he didn't have to miss work. He earned $400 a month at Finstad Heating and Sheet Metal; $50 a month went to his ex-wife, Teresa, mother of their two-year-old daughter. He said he lived at 240 S. Third, not far from the river, and not far from where he let Dick out of his car. They took a written statement from him. Then they remembered to ask him – did Doug know anything about Dick's coat? It was missing. He admitted that on October 12 he had found a coat in his car. It looked too small to belong to anyone he knew so he gave it to a nine-year-old neighbor boy. He said he would get it back for the detectives. No one asked why Doug had returned to the Everts' house after dropping Dick off downtown. Almost as an afterthought, the detectives asked about Pat Hockett. Juddi said Pat wasn't home, and had not been home the night of the party. District Attorney Frank Knight arrived at the house, and he and Montgomery questioned Mel. His story matched the others. If they asked him what had happened between Doug and Dick in the car, or where Dick was sitting when Mel climbed out and left the two alone, it wasn't noted.

At 1:40 a.m. on what was now October 22, the detectives went to the home of Marty Tucker. His parents were home and they got Marty out of bed and they all sat and talked in the living room. Marty knew his ride home only by his first name — Doug. Marty was in the right front seat during his ride home and had slid out through the driver's side door to get out. He said that at the time he was dropped off, Dick was sitting in the rear of the car, but he didn't remember which side. Mel was also in the back seat. Marty thought he arrived home a few minutes before his midnight curfew.

Marty's memory of the disturbance at the house was different than his hosts'. He said Paul had taken Dick out to the porch, there had been a scuffle, and Dick had not apologized and not reentered the house. He called it "not a real fight" but told detectives that Paul "had Kitchel by the front of the shirt and had just backed him up to the porch rail and no blows were exchanged." His parents said they had no objection to Marty taking a lie detector test.

Exactly what happened at the party? Who was angry enough to start or continue a fight with Dick on a dead quiet downtown street? The detectives would learn that some of the attendees were more than casual acquaintances. Juddi had had some kind of relationship with Doug. Maybe Paul knew, maybe he didn't. Maybe Dick knew and threw it in Paul's face. There was more than a casual argument on the front porch. Someone had left the party with a grudge against Dick. Did they follow Doug's car? Maybe Dick hitchhiked after he was left off and been murdered by an unknown person. Had he arrived home and had one last fight with his father? Why was Dick's jacket in Doug's car?

The stories about what happened at the party would change over the coming days. Dick's friends called him friendly, likeable, and, sadly, "unfinished." But more than one adult – friends or neighbors of his father – said sarcastically, "it couldn't happen to a better person" and "good riddance." One thing for sure: Dick *did* have an enemy.

THE SHOE STORE

Kitchel's Shoe Repair & Boot Shop ("Your Foot's Best Friend") smelled of old shoes and the people who wore them, with a strong whiff of polish. The aroma hit you as soon as you stepped into the store. I don't know how many times I went there on errands for my parents, but I know that not long after Dick was murdered, I took in some pumps and had them dyed lime green to go with a dress my mother and I had labored and cried over. I wore the shoes and the dress exactly once, to our high school winter formal, which students had voted to name "Christmas Carousel" since the spring musical was to be Rodgers and Hammerstein's *Carousel*.

I knew Dick a little from our three years at Western View Junior High School. He was in my eighth grade social studies class and signed two of my yearbooks. Despite his troubled home, or maybe because of it, he was one of the few boys to show up for picture-taking day in a shirt and tie. I remember him when he was sweet, and when he became what we called a JD, a juvenile delinquent.

You entered Kitchel's from an alley. Both Ralph Kitchel and Dick's stepmother, Sylvia, worked at the store. The shop shared a building at 4th and Madison with Leading Floral, which was co-owned by our family friends named, ironically, Plants. When I was about two years old and my brother, Sterling (called Terry as a child) was six, we posed in the window with Leading Floral's Christmas scene, sharing Santa's sleigh with him. It was the family Christmas card that year. Also on the same block as Kitchel's and Leading Floral was a fat girl's clothing store called Tots to Teens, and a dentist. My mother dragged me to both and together they are two of the most humiliating and painful memories of my childhood. I was "stocky" rather than fat, but she insisted that I wear a girdle in grade school and I was teased to no end in the locker room. Thank goodness I was tall for my age and usually placed in the back row for grade school photographs during my years at Roosevelt School.

A place I did like to spend time was Safeway, across the alley from Kitchel's. I hung out in a far corner of the grocery store where the magazines were. My mother thought I was looking at *Seventeen*, with the cute clothes and instructions for perfecting a flip hairstyle. But I was interested in a lot more than hairstyles and short skirts. While my mother shopped – I noticed she never looked at prices because she didn't have to – I studied *True Detective*, *True Crime*, *Women in Crime*, *Master Detective*, and others magazines with stories about bad people doing bad things. A bonus was the lurid crime scene photos. In the magazines, women could be one of two things – a damsel in distress, usually a dead one, or armed and dangerous. No question that sensuality led to murder. The police were always good guys, if a bit thuggish.

Safeway, Kitchel's, and Leading Floral were the triumvirate of my childhood. Plus our church, First Christian, was just a block west, so it was a familiar part of downtown. The other place that was important in my childhood was the KOAC radio studio on campus and later its TV studio, which my father, James Morris, known affectionately to all as Jimmie, managed.

I had never attended a funeral because by the time I was born all my grandparents were deceased. My parents were in their late thirties and mid-forties when they adopted Sterling, believing they couldn't have children; I was a surprise four years later. I did, however, see the inner workings of a funeral home. As soon as I had my driver's license, I began working holidays and funerals for Leading Floral. Mostly

I delivered flowers on busy days like Valentine's Day and Mother's Day. I dreaded Christmas Eve because it was sure to be dark and rainy and I would get lost on muddy country roads. Even on a good day, the flowers frequently tipped over in the van and would arrive at their destination dry and smooshed. I never admitted it; I just tried to get them to sit up straight again and encouraged the recipient to add some water as soon as possible.

I also delivered flowers to the funeral homes — DeMoss-Durdan, and McHenry. I did not deliver the flowers for Dick's funeral at McHenry, or run them out to where he was buried, at Twin Oaks Memorial Gardens & Mausoleum across the river in Albany. But at DeMoss-Durdan, where as a grade schooler I'd stood on the front steps under the white pillars and sung Christmas carols with my Roosevelt classmates, I often set up funeral sprays around the (usually) closed casket in a chapel. Then I'd wait in the basement while the funeral was conducted. Within seconds of the conclusion of the service, the floral arrangements were thrown down a chute. I'd catch them, quickly lay them in the back of the van, and speed out to the cemetery to set them around the grave before family and friends arrived. That was as close as I got to a funeral until the year after we graduated from high school, when Alan Murphy, the twin brother of my best friend Margret, died in a car accident on S. 3rd, or 99 W., the road leading south out of town. Montgomery and Hockema did not hold a high of opinion of Ralph Kitchel. They thought he was a drunk and knew he had a history of fighting with his son. They speculated that he might have served time in a penitentiary; in those days, that's where you learned a trade like shoe repair (like Alexandre Manette in *A Tale of Two Cities)*. Most shocking was that Kitchel did not seem sad about the murder of his only child. He was hostile to the police trying to solve his son's death but they saw no signs of grief. Not once did he phone them asking about progress on the case. "If it had been my child," Montgomery said later, "I would have been bugging all hell out of the police."

As a member of the rally squad, Judy Appelman took her tennis shoes to Kitchel's Shoe Repair that fall to be dyed Columbia Blue, the CHS school color. She saw Dick's father several times in the next few months. He knew that Dick had dated her. He'd told the police she was a friend of Dick's. They didn't talk about Dick when she visited the store. "He was so generous and so nice," Judy said, "but we all thought he had killed his son."

It was a commonly held assumption.

THE DETECTIVES
AND THE DA #1

Bill Hockema and Jim Montgomery spent most of their time investigating car thefts, stolen bikes, and noise complaints at fraternities. Corvallis was a small enough town that if there was a burglary, police could spot the work of local thieves and one of the detectives would say to the other, "You know, that sounds like so and so." They were invariably right.

Police records for the overnight hours of October 11 to October 12 show it was an ordinary shift for the four patrol officers on duty. While Dick was at the party, they responded to reports of four open windows, two open doors, one noise complaint, one suspicious vehicle, and one broken street light. It was also part of their routine to drive by and check out the small airport south of town and to drive through Avery Park.

The park was named for Joseph C. Avery, who in 1845 took out a land claim and built a home and a store where the mouth of the Mary's River flows into the Willamette. Part of Avery's land claim became a 75-acre park. In the 1950s and '60s, it was home to a small zoo, with monkeys, duck ponds, deer pens, and peacocks. There were slides, swings, teeter-totters, a jungle gym, and a merry-go-round. There were sports fields and a covered shelter where my dad's Lions Club held its annual picnic and where CHS mini-reunions, including those of the class of 1968, are held.

But the star of the park were the bears. They came and went – sometimes literally. More than once a bear escaped. The living conditions in the pit were deplorable. Bears died, new ones were acquired. Finally, the last, lonely bear at

Avery Park learned how to crawl up the side and hide in the nearby woods. Corvallis police were called out numerous times to help trap it until finally they were asked to get rid of it. A police officer took a rifle up to the park and shot it dead.

Corvallis is considering changing the name of Avery Park. In 2017, as the movement spread around the country to erase names connected with remnants of racism, a report by a group of scholars at OSU linked Avery to a pro-slavery newspaper in 1857-58. In addition to the park, the Avery name is on more than one street in town, a historic district, and two neighborhood associations. Avery also helped found the college and OSU has removed his name from one building.

There were few violent or suspicious deaths in the history of the town and they were quickly wrapped up. In 1952, a twenty-year-old man got into a fight with the husband of a woman he was seeing. The two men fought and the younger one stabbed the husband to death. It was ruled was self-defense, he was freed, and he later married the widow, a mother of six children. Over the years, there was a boy who was slapped to death, a girl who was starved to death, and quarrels between lovers. In 1955, a resident of Alsea, a small, unincorporated area of Benton County, west of Corvallis, came home late one night and sat in his living room with a gun. It went off. A bullet went into the ceiling and struck and killed his two-year-old stepdaughter sleeping upstairs. It was labeled an accident. In 1965, a sixteen-year-old boy strangled his girlfriend at Irish Bend, a spot on the Willamette River sixteen miles south of town, near Monroe. The murder charge against him was reduced to manslaughter. The police department itself was pretty much scandal free, except for an incident in the 1950s. A few officers took advantage of an "open door" policy at Montgomery Ward on 2nd Street, the same building that hosted KKK dances. The open door meant that the store looked the other way if a police officer just happened to walk out with merchandise.

A few officers were fired when the thefts were brought to the police chief's attention. Drugs started to show up in Corvallis in the late 1960s and early 1970s, mostly marijuana. One day, a security guard responsible for manning an entrance to the OSU campus caught a whiff of marijuana in a car full of students. The guard happened to have been raised in Nebraska and knew the odor of hemp. He called the city police. It was the town's very first drug bust.

Montgomery and Hockema had never had a case they didn't close. Jim Montgomery was thirty-five years old, a detective sergeant, and was known as the good cop when he was paired with Bill Hockema. Not that either of them would rough up a suspect. Montgomery worked a lot of sex crimes, and had a reputation for getting confessions and convictions. He had joined the Corvallis Police Department in July 1957 and was the father of two young children. Bill Hockema was thirty-three, had joined the force a year earlier, and was a captain in charge of detectives. He had attended the FBI Academy in 1964 in order to advance, and earn more money, in the Corvallis Police Department. He had four young children. Hockema's bad cop routine was mostly talking tough. Assistant Chief Ken Burright was in his forties, several years older than his detectives, and the father of three. An army veteran of World War II, he had seen a lot and suspected that the Kitchel murder was going to be a difficult case to solve.

It wasn't pleasant for any of them to view Dick's body. As fathers, they didn't like to see anyone die young. But they had been called to the scene of auto accidents that were more gruesome than finding Dick in the river.

It was important for Montgomery and Hockema to move quickly, while Dick's friends were still learning of his death and their memories were fresh. Rumors were already reaching the detectives. Dick had been killed by a gang from Albany, a town on the other side of the Willamette River. He was the target of a mob hit. Drugs were involved. He was killed by kids from Junction City who were cruising Corvallis the night of October 11. Two groups of drunk boys were seen throwing a boy into the river; no one saw him get out. Some people believed someone at the party carrying a grudge followed Dick and killed him. Most thought that Dick and his father had had one too many fights, and his father had accidentally killed his son and hid his body in the river.

The detectives walked two blocks east to the district attorney's office regularly to update him on the Kitchel investigation, or they would corral Frank Knight if he was at the police department. Knight was their loyal defender as well as their nemesis. It would be Knight who decided if anyone would be charged with Dick's death. Time and again, Montgomery and Hockema would make their case to Knight about one particular suspect; time after time, he said there wasn't enough evidence.

Knight had arrived in Corvallis in 1963 to become a deputy district attorney. He was just one year out of the Willamette University College of Law, the father of two young children, and handsome with a thick shock of black hair and black framed glasses. He knew District Attorney Al Joiner was not going to run for re-election, and Knight positioned himself as Joiner's successor. Knight was elected DA in 1965 and 1968. Knight's office was on the third floor of the west side of the Benton County Courthouse, the pride of Corvallis since 1888. The courthouse, four stories with an impressive stairway leading to the front door, has a red roof and is known for its spire which houses a gigantic clock visible from all four sides. Until 1953, the clock was wound twice a week by hand by a maintenance man who had to climb into the tower and manually raise 650 pounds of weights which kept the clock working. It's the only pioneer courthouse in Oregon still used for its original purpose.

The three would sit in Knight's office and discuss the interviews they had conducted with Dick's friends and his parents, and the polygraph tests they wanted done. They talked scenarios. "We knew Ralph Kitchel had a temper," Knight said later. "One of the things we had to keep in mind was that Dick might have gone home and his father had killed him. He was a serious question mark in the case." While Knight for the most part accepted the results of the autopsy on Dick, he had reservations about the man who conducted it, State Medical Examiner Dr. Russell Henry. Knight thought Henry had a history of being too quick to settle on strangulation as a cause of death. But Knight agreed that Dick was killed the night of the party and put immediately into the river.

Knight controlled any and all information that reached the press. What he didn't want was a city where the police could speak directly to newspapers and radio stations. "You don't want that when you've got a case under investigation," he said. Experience had taught him that you "couldn't keep the police shut up" if information was permitted to flow through them. Later in the fall, the *Gazette-Times* would compare Knight and the handling of the Kitchel case to Salem, Oregon, police – just 40 miles north of Corvallis – which *did* share information with the press, against the wishes of its DA. Knight defended his approach by explaining he was worried about pre-trial publicity and protecting the rights of the accused. "An irresponsible press," Knight was quoted as saying, "could use [information] in a way to defeat justice and disregard the rights of the accused."

The Kitchel case would test Knight's working relationship with the press in Corvallis, and the one person responsible for coverage of the murder in the *Gazette-Times*, Mike Bradley.

MONDAY

On the first school day after Dick's body was found, his death was mentioned in the morning announcements delivered over the public address system at CHS. It was two days since his body had floated near the dock of Riverview Marina, and the day before his funeral. If it happened today, counselors would be brought to school. There would be vigils. An outpouring of media coverage. Television interviews with his friends and parents. Pleas for people to come forward and provide information. That kind of media intensity didn't exist then. There was nothing except well-meaning but incomplete coverage by our local paper, the *Gazette-Times*. Some of Dick's friends already knew about his death because word had spread, and some had already been interviewed by the police. I remember hearing the announcement on the PA system and how surreal it seemed. I have no memory of discussing Dick's death with others at school, or with my parents. They may have assumed I didn't know him. All over town, parents weren't talking to their teenagers about the boy who had been murdered. They just let it be. But Dick's friends were talking to each other.

I was reading newspapers and asking questions by the time I could walk, so the *G-T* and *The Oregonian* would have been my source for details. It wasn't our high school newspaper. I was on the staff of the *High-O-Scope*. We didn't mention Dick's murder, presumably because our bi-weekly was distributed every other Friday inside the *G-T*. But our memories are hazy. I've checked mine with Donella Russell, who was editor of the *High-O-Scope* and a friend of mine since kindergarten days at Roosevelt School, as well as Blue

Birds and Camp Fire. She says it is possible we were told not to write about Dick. The next spring, Alice Henderson, the editor of the yearbook, wanted to do a full page about Dick; the administration told her no. She found a way and did it anyway.

On Monday, Montgomery and Hockema made the first of several visits to Corvallis High School to talk to students and faculty. They met with Robert Payne, the new assistant principal who had taught American History, coached basketball, and served as athletic director before moving into administration. The detectives pulled various boys and girls out of class to speak to them in Payne's office. It was the first time they had met Diana Eddins, the girl who had been with Dick on Labor Day weekend when he had been arrested for drinking, crashing his car, and resisting arrest. That was their second date; they never had another.

"He was a cute guy, not very big," she remembers. On their first date, they hung out at Seaton's and he got to second base, she told me. She had heard rumors about his drinking and on their next date they went to a party north of town and both got drunk. Just before they crashed on 9th Street, not far from Seaton's, she thought about trying to take the keys out of the ignition but was afraid that would make things worse. They knew a police car was following them and Dick sped up and swerved over to the wrong side of the street. They crashed into a row of mailboxes, trees, and a fence. They were taken to the police station and Diana was put in a room by herself. "My dad is going to kill me," she thought to herself. Her parents, Helen and Larry Eddins, "good people" according to their daughter, grounded her for the rest of the year. She stayed friends with Dick but they never had another date, and he wasn't permitted to phone her. Then she heard that he was dead. "I didn't cry – I was shocked," she remembered.

The picture the detectives got was that on the night of the Everts' party, Dick had been spoiling for a fight. He had told friends that he wanted to fight various boys who for one reason or another – or no reason – irritated him. He imagined fights between others too. Judy Appelman remembered that Dick would ask friends to fight for him. Usually they shrugged it off. Dick wanted a friend to fight Paul Everts for him, because Paul had shoved Dick around at an earlier party. Recently, Dick had been in a fight with Mike Nader, who thought Dick was flirting with his girl, the babysitter who lived at the Everts'.

Detectives also spoke to another vice principal at CHS, Charles Kipper. From him they learned about Roger Bicks, Dick's stepbrother, who had a violent temper and had been expelled for non-attendance. Roger was also living at 301 Bell Lane with Dick, Ralph, Sylvia, and a brother. The school administrators knew Dick and his stepbrother had problems living under the same roof. Roger had spent more time in Cottage Grove than in Corvallis, and the detectives made a note to talk to authorities there.

Montgomery and Hockema met with Bob Wadlow, who drove Dick to the party on October 11 and never saw him again. He couldn't tell them much about Dick's state of mind that night. The detectives asked all the students they interviewed about who might have had a grudge against Dick, and compiled a long list of who was arguing with whom.

One of the boys the detectives talked to at the school had been at the party and witnessed the argument between Dick and Paul. He described Paul grabbing Dick by the shirt collar, but had not seen how the argument ended. He did see them walk back into the house together. The detectives heard more rumors flying around, including a tip that Dick had been seen after being let out of Doug's car. They never pinned that one down.

Mel Plemmons, whom they talked with briefly when they broke the news about Dick's body being found to the partygoers at the Everts', showed up at the police station to see them where he could talk more freely. He told the detectives more about the fighting. Telling much the same story as Judy Appelman had, he explained that in Dick's social group one member would carry a grudge, announce they were going to have a fight and who with, then, in Dick's case, ask someone to fight it for them. He also said Dick was angry at Paul long before October 11.

They talked to Terry Garren, class of 1967, who was at the party. Terry said news of an upcoming party at the Everts' would be shared by word of mouth. The Everts liked young people around, and the teenagers contributed money to the keggers. Terry had gone to Harding and Garfield grade schools and knew Dick. Dick was "a drunk, feisty little guy" and much smaller than Terry. Dick had asked him once if he wanted to fight. Terry laughed at him. Terry also knew Doug and his brother and sometimes fished with them. Terry never told his parents he was at the party the evening Dick disappeared. He thought of contacting the police, but they found him before he could. Terry lived next door to Mel, and tried to talk with Mel about Dick's disappearance and murder, but Mel wouldn't talk about it. "Everybody was pretty scared" about Dick's murder, Terry said later. "They pointed fingers at everybody else." To this day, Terry has a vivid mental picture of the party. "It was crowded. Dick was swearing at everybody." Dick picked a fight with a boy and Terry broke it up, telling the boy, "Come on, he's drunk, he's not really wanting to fight." Terry said he thought Dick was so drunk that he didn't know what he was doing.

Mel did speak to Terry once about the evening. He was the one who told Terry "they can't find Dick."

Monday afternoon, Montgomery and Hockema drove Paul and Juddi Everts, Doug Hamblin, and Marty Tucker to the Eugene Police Department for polygraphs. The detectives liked to drive because it sent a message that the police were in charge and guaranteed the exams would happen. The time in the car might also encourage conversation on the way down or back. The detectives usually took a few minutes before the exams to talk to the examiner and suggest questions. Juddi was not given a polygraph. Instead, in the weeks that followed, the detectives found several opportunities to talk with her alone.

The polygraph examiner found Marty to be "a nervous young man, somewhat agitated when discussing the events leading up to the night of the death of the victim." The examiner concluded that Marty's stress and vagueness was caused by his being underage and not wanting to admit that he had been drinking. Marty mentioned that he saw Dick with Paul after the altercation and Dick did not appear to be hurt in any way.

They asked Paul some baseline questions, including if he had ever stolen anything. He answered no. When he was told there was a problem with his response, he admitted he had taken some candy as a child. "I was really nervous," he said later. He thought he had told the police everything he knew. There had been a fight between Dick and Doug on the front porch. He didn't know what it was about. It wasn't "a big brawl." He didn't remember if Dick ever reentered the house.

The report on his polygraph examination read:

The subject is quite friendly, intelligent, seemingly candid, young man. He states that he was friends with the victim, that he feels it incumbent upon himself to help the police in any possible what that he can, to determine who it was caused the victim's death. He states he feels quite strongly about this matter, and cannot talk too long about the death of the victim without becoming slightly emotional about it.

As is common with polygraph tests, Paul was asked two sets of questions, both general ones and specific ones, and was asked both sets twice for comparison's sake. The specific ones were very specific: Had he thrown the victim's body in the river? Did he know who did? Had he hit the victim in the face or throat? He answered all "no." The examiner concluded that "this subject is not deceptive … the answers given in response to the questions listed are truthful."

Like the others, Paul didn't know until he read in the *Gazette-Times* the next day that he was mentioned as among those taking a polygraph tests. Paul's parents were living in Cincinnati but subscribed to the *G-T.* He called to warn them that they would see his name in the newspaper.

District Attorney Frank Knight was quoted in the newspaper as saying that it appeared the group was being truthful to police. But he was not sharing all he knew. The polygraph examination of Doug had followed the same format – two sets of questions asked twice. He was asked if he'd had a fight with the victim, if he knew who choked the victim, and if *he* had choked the victim and thrown the body in the river. The examiner wrote that the results of Doug's test were "inconclusive" and it was "highly desirable" that he be re-examined.

THE SCHOOL

The week Dick's body was found coincided with Spirit Week at CHS. When the detectives went to the school to hold interviews, they were conducting serious business in an atmosphere of pep rallies, assemblies, a spaghetti-eating contest, a dance, and a bonfire, all leading up to Homecoming.

Alice Henderson was one of the princesses on the Homecoming Court and her date would, naturally, be Tom Norton. To me, they were the golden couple. She was tall and slender and extremely pretty with short dark hair and freckles. He was lean and cute. They seemed impossibly busy. Alice's father was Assistant Director of the Agricultural Experiment Station at OSU and most likely, he and my father knew each other because an important part of KOAC's programming was agricultural related. How else would farmers across Oregon find out about the weather and crop prices than by radio? Alice was editor of the yearbook and Tom was one of the photographers. They had been dating since they were juniors, but not going 'steady,' so both occasionally went to school events with others.

I was not in their circle of friends, so it was easy to believe they had lives with few problems. I didn't know that Alice was making important choices that came after long thought, and that Tom kept busy because he was, as he described later, "hiding." Alice had been selected for rally squad at Western View Junior High, but dropped it because she "felt unsophisticated in the world of dating, which seemed to be part of the cheerleading life." She began to focus on journalism and yearbook. She spent the summer before our senior year as an exchange student in Japan, seeing the extremes of life there. She lived and traveled with a wealthy Japanese family, but also spent one week working alongside a family who farmed rice paddies. When she returned to Corvallis, she spoke at a school assembly and at grade schools and service clubs around town. But something was missing. She felt like she came home with a lot of stories and no peers or friends to tell them to. The two and a half months had changed her. She had attended the First Methodist Church with her family all of her life, but she began to think about what she believed or didn't believe about faith and about her purpose in life.

Both Alice and Tom knew Dick only on a nodding acquaintance. We all attended Western View Junior High where our ninth grade class numbered about 250. Our CHS graduating class would be more than twice as many students. We were separated by the courses we were placed in: either Basic, AP (Advanced Placement), or CP (College Prep). I'm not sure how that worked because sometimes I was with the smart kids and sometimes I wasn't. Tom and Dick had something in common in junior high and in high school – an eagerness to be so friendly that they knew everyone and everyone knew them. For Dick, his friends were his family; knowing a lot of people helped Tom to hide.

Tom spent his high school years staying busy because he was "running away from my shadow," he said later. "I wanted to be everybody's friend and know everybody's name. I was in so much pain." Tom had a clear memory of when he knew he was different. When he was five years old, he was riding in the family's 1950 Mercury. He heard a radio announcer say a minister had been arrested in Salem for homosexual relations. Tom asked his mother what a homosexual was. "When she told me, I thought, that's me!" he recalled. "I wanted to slide into the crack in the seat." After that, anytime Tom heard a siren or saw a patrol car, he worried the police were coming for him. He worried the rest of his childhood. He dealt by getting good grades and getting a girlfriend.

Some days he daydreamed of different ways of committing suicide. He fantasized driving down a highway and "falling asleep" at the wheel or freezing to death in the wilderness. He shared his pain with no one. CHS had five counselors to help us with our academic and personal problems. He went to see one of the men on staff, but never confided what he was troubled over. He cared about Alice, and they were mostly going steady but she was a "safe date." "She wasn't going to expect me to be sexually aggressive with her," he said. "I was naïve about homosexuality. I thought if I had a girlfriend, I could change." He didn't tell her about his orientation because he didn't want to lose her as a friend. He was formulating a plan that would be sure to make a man of him. He would join the army.

Of course, Tom was not the only gay student. Stan Selfridge said that being a gay teenager in Corvallis wasn't much fun. He had a few friends in junior high and high school, boys he could be himself with. One of them was Tom. Like Tom, Stan kept busy, with Future Business Leaders of America and other school leadership roles. In ninth grade, Tom and Stan were co-student managers of the basketball team at Western View. "I never searched out anyone to talk to about being gay," Stan said. "I just lived my life." Stan dated some girls, one who has remained a close friend.

For Spirit Week, we seniors nominated Mark Goheen as our biggest eater. "I had a reputation for that," he said later. The entire student body met in the gym and while the varsity rally squad led cheers of "Go, Mark, Go!" and "Eat, Mark, Eat!", Mark and two other boys representing the junior and sophomore classes ate cold, sticky spaghetti made the night before. At some point, Mark remembers, "The three of us looked at each other and said, 'We've got to stop this.'" They did, and Mark was declared the winner. "The senior class went nuts. I felt miserable for two days."

We had gone to one of about a dozen elementary schools in Corvallis and surrounding rural areas, and one of two junior high schools. We were one of the last classes to attend high school together. A second high school opened three years after we graduated. My mother and her brothers and sisters had attended the original CHS on 6th between Monroe and Madison which opened in 1910-11 on what was called the school blocks, now Central Park.

There were about 1,800 of us attending the "new" three year high school, built in an art deco style at 11th Street and Buchanan in 1935, then on the far northwest edge of town. Over the years, a science and library wing, as well as the cafeteria and large gym, were added. Dixon Creek, where a young cousin of mine drowned in the early 1940s, ran near the school. We called it Crud Creek and once a year did a quick sweep and clean-up of it.

We were smart. We had more students in the top one percent of the country's high schools than any other town in Oregon. We had smart teachers – most of them had graduate degrees. We were responsible so there was no formal dress code or closed campus, as some high schools were experimenting with. Girls wore skirts or dresses, and panty hose or knee socks, and few boys had long hair. If you smoked, you politely stepped across the street. We could come and go in our cars. We were smug, especially those of us with parents at OSU, believing we were better than the teenagers who lived on the other side of the rivers to the south and east of us. Dick was one of the boys who took auto mechanic and shop classes, but he was friends with many who were in CP and AP courses.

We were conventional. Many girls took typing and business courses because, as our yearbook reminded us, those classes "prepare a student for the role of a secretary or businessman." We had dozens of clubs, and many in 1967-68 split along gender lines. The Future Farmers of America club was composed of about three dozen boys.

Future Homemakers of America was made up of less than a dozen girls, but the membership of Future Teachers of America and Future Business Leaders of America were evenly split between boys and girls. My mother had learned the hard way that a woman should be able to support herself. When my grandfather deserted the family, my grandmother ran a boarding house for OSU students, and later was a housekeeper and restaurant cook. My mother's goal was for me to be a hair stylist. I had bigger dreams. I had been writing since childhood, and by a young age, had a box full of short stories I had submitted, unsuccessfully, to children's magazines, and a few plays I had written. I didn't know where writing would take me, but I'm grateful every day she insisted I learn to type.

I had been in band since sixth grade, a middling player of the alto sax. When I was a senior, band conflicted with journalism so I dropped band and threw myself into work on the *High-O-Scope*. The other advantage to not being in band was that I didn't have to try and fit into a boy's band uniform, with no room for hips or breasts. Except for Donella Russell, who was the editor, and the business manager and ad manager, we rotated jobs on the paper, but most weeks my name appeared as a member of the editorial board. Instead of the usual reporting, including attending student council meetings – that fall, it was debating if the school needed an anonymous suggestion box for students to tell the administration our uncensored thoughts – I created a regular feature in which I would select students representing each grade and get them together to talk about what I thought were the subjects of the day. Now I laugh at my pretentiousness. One week the headline on my feature read Sex and the Cinema Today: A Panel Discussion by Youth. Another week it was Smoking Among Teenagers: Hazardous or Harmless? I imagine I was playing with alliteration. And then there was the always relevant: Grades: What Do They Mean and Are They Really Important? followed a few months later by a feature on a pass-fail grading system. Later in the year there were pages devoted to Does Corvallis Have a Marijuana Problem? and an interview with Police Chief James Goodman. His answer was, "It depends on one's definition of a problem." There was a sidebar summing up interviews with a few students about their experience with pot. The conclusions we printed added up to "don't try it."

I'm sure some were experimenting. But I had never had a drink of alcohol, smoked a cigarette, or tried marijuana. I was grounded – a lot – but for being stubborn, taking the car when I wasn't supposed to, and did I mention I was stubborn?

Depending on the week and a rotation of jobs, I was busy writing articles, selling ads, and serving on the editorial board. Because I had a car – my parents' 1959 Ford Galaxy, which I scraped on a metal pole at Seaton's – I could run down to the *G-T,* then at the southwest corner of 3rd and Jefferson, for last minute tasks and give rides to others on the newspaper staff. The *G-T* kindly let us use what was called the Barometer Room, a space with typewriters and desks designated for use by the OSU's *Daily Barometer.* The *High-O-Scope* staff was responsible for every step of the process, not just writing stories and taking photographs, but working with linotype operators, an early computer, preparing photos for printing, and correcting galley proofs until the presses rolled, literally. I was also on the debate team and remember that at one competition I had to speak on capital punishment. I don't remember if I was for it or against it.

I didn't know it at the time, but many students couldn't wait to graduate and leave town. "I didn't want to spend ten minutes more there than I had to," Donella says now. Her mother had a degree in botany and her father was a landscape architect. Together they ran Russell's Green Thumb Nursery. Donella was the oldest of eleven children (including birth siblings, cousins, and foster children) and often it was her job to cook for the family. "We had no money, but I loved books." And she had them. "My mother never met an encyclopedia salesman she didn't like," she remembers. Donella wanted to see the world and was focused on reading about other countries and someday traveling. She worked at the soda fountain inside the Memorial Union on the OSU campus, helped at banquets, and sometimes worked at the town's cannery.

The racial makeup of our class was pretty much like the town. We were overwhelmingly white. There was one student in our senior class and one faculty member who were African American. The school and town weren't much of an adjustment for our exchange student, who came from Cape Town, South Africa, where life was segregated. She told the *High-O-Scope* that the "only dark person I ever really got to know was our maid." There was a handful of Asian Americans, and two students whose families had fled the Netherlands Indies (now Indonesia) after World War II.

My family's church, First Christian, sponsored the Van Gents and I grew up with their son, Ron. The Federated Churches, the First Presbyterian, and Congregational churches brought the Niggebrugge family to Corvallis. I became good friends with Linda Niggebrugge, who arrived in town with her parents and two sisters in the early 1950s. The girls were placed in classes one year back because of the new language, but in three months, they were speaking English. Linda's parents did not adjust. Each had grown up wealthy in the Netherlands Indies in families that owned sugar plantations, drove Bentleys, owned race horses, and attended the opera. Both of Linda's parents were interred or in prison during the war when the Netherlands surrendered to the Japanese. After the war and after the children were born, the family lived in The Hague, until they followed Linda's grandfather to Oregon. Nothing in Corvallis compared and Linda's parents emotionally abandoned their children. Her mother quit making breakfast for her daughters, never read or told another story, stopped playing music, and spent years crying. Her father wanted to return to Holland but her mother refused, "so we were all miserable together," Linda said later. He became emotionally cruel to this daughters.

I knew nothing of this. What I knew was I had a dark-skinned friend with braids to her waist. Mine only reached my shoulders. We were in nearly every class together at Roosevelt and spent many afternoons running around the yard playing cowboys and Indians. Those were the years I was fascinated with our first television set and, in particular, Westerns. Although another Corvallis church had brought the family to town, I think my mother had befriended the Niggebrugges. It's something she would have done.

Today, our senior class seems to have had an unusual lack of diversity for a high school in a college town. But for decades Oregon State University attracted students studying agriculture, forestry, and engineering. The university didn't have an international faculty until decades later. In 1958, OSU boasted that it had 207 international students from 36 different countries. Most did not have children in the school system.

The highlight of Spirit Week was when Alice Henderson was crowned Homecoming Queen. In a photograph on the front page of the *High-O-Scope,* she is wearing a small tiara and carrying a bouquet of roses. She is covering her mouth with one gloved hand, looking wide-eyed and very surprised at the announcement. Tom Norton is looking on proudly, smiling and leaning toward her to study her reaction. CHS lost the big football game to Lebanon, 27-0.

THE REPORTER

Mike Bradley didn't take well to Frank Knight's withholding news about the Kitchel murder. Like an annoying pebble in a shoe, Bradley was an irritating presence Knight couldn't shake clear of. In truth, neither man had much experience with murder. They had that in common, even if they didn't realize it.

When covering an important story, Bradley was in the habit of dropping by pertinent city or county offices. The best information was gathered in person, not on the phone. It only took a few minutes for him to walk from the offices of the *G-T,* downtown at 3rd and Jefferson, to City Hall, at 5th and Madison, to the Benton County offices in the courthouse at 120 NW. 4th, and to the police department, which was in the old Southern Pacific Depot by the train tracks at 6th and Madison and kitty-corner from our church. But Knight kept a lid on what was shared. "In those days, reporters would sit around a police station, chat with officers," Knight said. That's what he didn't want to happen. He thought it could hamper an investigation. It wasn't until years later that news conferences with law enforcement were broadcast and a victim's family could speak to cameras and microphones and plead for information from the public.

After shrugging off Dick's disappearance for a few days, Ralph Kitchel had contacted the Corvallis Police Department on Tuesday, October 17. He went in person and took along a photograph of Dick. A form titled Missing/Found Person Report includes a brief description of Dick's clothing: he was last seen wearing his tan, suede, sheep-lined jacket, blue jeans, and cowboy boots. Someone had jotted down some of the names of people at the party and a few of Dick's friends. Judy Appelman's name was included, with a note that she was a girlfriend of the missing teen. There's a mention that Dick was friends with a CHS shop teacher. There's also a mention of one boy who had been seen crying at school. Maybe he knew something. The report stated that Dick's father had agreed to the newspaper and radio stations being notified of the disappearance. The form said the cause of absence was "possibly fear of upcoming court date." There is also a mention that Dick's mother, Joan Borden, who lived in Olympia, Washington, had phoned to speak with the police.

Bradley probably first heard of the missing teenager via a routine news release, mailed or handed to the reporter when he made one of his visits, or it may have been sent to the newspaper soon after Ralph Kitchel reported him missing. A story about Dick's being missing ran on October 20 in the *Gazette-Times*. The headline read Missing Youth Being Sought. The story said that Dick was due to appear in municipal court that same day "to face serious traffic charges" and suggested maybe he wasn't so much missing as he was ducking out on facing the music. "It is believed that fear of appearing in court might have influenced his disappearance," it read. The story, with no byline, ended by asking people who might know his whereabouts to contact his parents – not the police department, his parents – which seems unusual and a sign the police department agreed with Ralph Kitchel that Dick was a runaway.

His body was found the next day, Saturday, October 21, and news coverage was now the purveyance of Mike Bradley. Bradley was fifty-one years old and had been at the *G-T* for twenty-one years. During a long career at the paper, he worked at nearly every job, but was best known as a city and county beat reporter. He took his work seriously – some elected officials thought *too* seriously – and did not always hide his opinions. In the mid-1950s, he had a column in the paper called "Off the Beat," in which he good-naturedly poked fun at the offices and people he wrote about on his "beat." He liked to point out some of the curious ways of local government, but always in the interest of making a point. In one column published on September 1, 1955, he talked about how twenty brass spittoons removed from courthouse halls after decades of use were quietly being sold off to be replaced by four "modern sand urns." Some of the spittoons had even mysteriously disappeared. A few weeks later, he teased the Benton County Clerk's office for painting its office walls "boudoir pink." But he also reported on more serious irregularities he spotted. For example: why had the county called for bids on *some* courthouse remodeling projects, but not others? In February 1956, he noted that the reason the courthouse had gone dark for a day was that bigger and more powerful lights had been installed, but no one thought to check to see if the wiring could accommodate the wattage. It couldn't.

To many in the community, he was best known for his conviction that government should conduct the public's business in public. That made him an occasional thorn in the side of the police and other city and county agencies, including DA Frank Knight's office. Montgomery and Hockema investigated Dick Kitchel's murder, but it was the DA who would decide if or when there was enough evidence to charge someone with murder.

Bradley had receding hair and was often photographed pushing up his black framed glasses with his left hand as he balanced a cigar. Like others who found themselves in journalism in those years, he had an unusual background. He got his taste for what would become his career writing for his high school newspaper in Seattle. But during the Depression, he worked as a cowboy and rodeo rider in eastern Oregon. He went back home to get a degree in journalism from the University of Washington, married, and moved to Corvallis to work for the *G-T* in 1946. He was a volunteer firefighter and painted landscapes and seascapes in his spare time.

A lot happened between the Missing Youth Being Sought story and the next one. In general, a story with no byline is based on a news release. A story with a byline has additional reporting. On Monday, October 23, Bradley's first bylined story on the murder ran on the top right of the front page. The front page is called a newspaper's "front door" because its layout communicates to readers what the most important stories are. Dick's death was the lead story. A large headline read: Missing Prep Student Found Murdered – River Gives Up Strangled Body of Richard Kitchel. The murder, Bradley wrote, was under "intense police investigation." The article mentioned the party Dick had been to on October 11 and even named some of those who had been in attendance: Paul Everett [sic], Mrs. Everett [sic], Marty Tucker, Mel Plemmons, and a "19 year old girl identified only as Pat." It stated that Doug Hamblin said he had let Dick out of his car downtown at about 1:30 a.m. Death was caused by strangulation following a fight. Time of death was determined to be in the early morning hours of October 12. The article stated that the people who had been at the party the last night of Dick's life had agreed to take a polygraph test. The article also mentioned that Dick had been in trouble with police in the past, and had drunk driving and hit and run charges pending against him.

A photograph of Dick wearing an OSU t-shirt, possibly the one he was wearing when he was found in the river, accompanied the article. It was his senior class photo. Dick's friends and classmates took offense at Bradley's story, in particular the mention that Dick had been arrested earlier that fall. They didn't think it was important and didn't think it was worth mentioning that he had been at a party the last night of his life.

On October 27, Linda Bigham, CHS class of 1967, wrote to the newspaper:

After all, Dick is dead and what could his past or present police record possibly accomplish now by being brought out except to dampen his character in the eyes of others.

Her letter, printed as a Readertorial, was titled Superfluous Paragraph. The following day, another Readertorial was published, titled Poor Taste.

The information given was most misleading and unsympathetic towards the deceased's character. Had this been a prominent businessman's or educator's son your parting eulogy would have been far different.

The letter was signed by 111 classmates, including Judy Appelman and the boys who were among the last to see him alive: Marty, Mel, and Bob.

Both letters asked the newspaper to apologize to his grieving parents and friends. There was no response from the newspaper. Newspapers generally let readers have their say without commenting. Bradley and the *G-T* saw Dick's history with the police as important to the article and possibly germane to his murder, a decision I agree with.

Dick had also made the *G-T* on September 1, but being a minor, was not named in a story about his wild ride and crash on N. 9th.

Just as there had been no media presence at the school after the murder, there were no articles in the *G-T* about Dick that told readers more about him. There were no stories about his Cub Scout years or love of baseball. In Dick's case, a sympathetic story would have been based on quotes from friends, one or two teachers, and a couple of stepmothers. Murder was huge news in Corvallis. Most were solved quickly. The feature stories we are familiar with today, which humanize the victim, were not common at the time. And not everyone saw Dick as a victim. There were more than a few in the community who thought Dick had gotten what was coming to him.

There were several more stories about Dick's murder over the next few weeks. One was about funeral services.

Another was the report that several people had been cleared by lie detector tests. One said there was nothing new in the investigation, recapped Dick's murder and where and when he was found, and quoted Frank Knight. He continued to be tight-lipped and careful about what he shared with Bradley. "He liked to sensationalize," Knight said years later of Bradley. "He wanted to stir something up." Which, incidentally, I can understand. Just as much as the police or prosecutor want to know what happened, so does a good reporter. For the most part, we rely on others for information. Since Knight had made the police off limits, everything Bradley wrote depended on what he could get out of the district attorney.

Knight felt pressure from Bradley. "He wanted me to say police were 'baffled' by the Kitchel murder," Knight said. "I would not tell him the police were 'baffled.'"

THE PARENTS

Sylvia Kitchel was no shrinking violet. Like Ralph, her husband of just six months, she was tough. "I know my rights!" she said more than once when she felt Detectives Hockema and Montgomery were hounding her and Ralph about submitting to a polygraph.

The couple's relationship with the police began routinely enough. On Monday, October 23, before they drove the first batch of Dick's friends and acquaintances to Eugene to take polygraphs, Montgomery and Hockema visited Ralph and Sylvia Kitchel at their home on Bell Lane. It was two days after Dick's body had been found, and the day before his funeral. Also present was Sylvia's son, Roger Bicks, and another man, described as a friend of the family. Another son of Sylvia's also lived at the house.

Hockema and Montgomery wanted to hear the parents' story again. Dick's father explained that he had last seen his son on October 11, when Dick had been picked up at the house by Bob Wadlow. The detectives asked Ralph why he had not reported Dick missing until Monday, October 16, a question that Ralph would balk at and be defensive about for months to come. Ralph said that one of the five days had been a teacher's in-service day, so no school, and then there was a weekend. Dick often went to the coast with friends and would stay away for several days. Ralph hadn't worried until Dick, whom his father called Richard, hadn't shown up for school on Monday.

They asked if Dick and had any enemies; his father said no. He offered that Dick was often involved in fights, "as any teenager would be," but he couldn't imagine a fight serious enough that it would result in a grudge and lead to murder. Someone had told the detectives that Paul Everts might have owed Dick money for helping with a move. Ralph confirmed that Dick had helped Paul out, but didn't know if he'd been paid yet or not.

The detectives began dropping in unannounced to the shoe repair store. Ralph and Sylvia did not like that. Maybe because Montgomery and Hockema never heard from Ralph, they would stop by to ask if the parents had heard anything new. Unfortunately for Ralph, who didn't seem to have a need to keep in contact with the police, the store was within a block or two of the police station, the courthouse, and the *G-T.*

"Ralph didn't like the police," Hockema said later. "He was upset with us for not solving the murder right away, and not ruling him out. But he was not sad." Privately, the detectives shook their heads over that. As fathers themselves, they knew they would be out of their minds if one of their children were missing, then found dead.

Sylvia was upset with them too. "You should let the sheriff's office investigate the murder. All the high school kids hate you," Sylvia told them. It was unclear if the hard feelings were the result of Dick's drunk driving accident and arrest a few weeks prior, or were the result of something else.

They knew Ralph had a temper. There was the history of police calls to the house to break up fights between Ralph and Dick. When they asked Ralph for a scenario – what did he think had happened the night of October 11? – Ralph told them that he thought the killing must have been an accident. Then the killer, still unknown, had panicked and thrown the body into the river. He was adamant that Dick had no enemies.

They learned quickly that Ralph Kitchel wasn't the kind of father who would hound them about his son's murder. He was angry, at them and everyone else, but didn't call or show up at the police department to plead for information on who killed his son or the status of the investigation. They didn't know what to make of him, and couldn't rule him out as a suspect. But they also couldn't prove that Dick had made it home that night and had one last fist fight with his father.

Ralph Kitchel was forty years old when his only child was murdered. He'd been born in 1928 in Pasco, Washington, and was one of four children raised by a widowed mother. A photo taken at about the time Ralph joined the navy in 1945 shows a young man with a long, narrow face, a large smile, and curly, sandy hair. You can see a resemblance to Dick in his eyes.

When Ralph had married Dick's mother Joan Carey in 1950, she was four months pregnant. After they divorced, she moved back to Washington. His second marriage was to Irene Kitchel, who bartended at the Peacock Tavern on 2nd Street. They divorced and he married Sylvia in the spring of 1967. It was her third or fourth marriage. By then, he had grown his shoe repair business from the back of the Acme shoe store on 2nd Street to its own storefront off the alley behind Leading Floral at 4th and Madison. He was known as a gruff man except with his friends at the American Legion, the Eagles Lodge, and the Moose Lodge.

Something had soured Ralph on life. Would Dick have grown up to be his father? Maybe not. Ralph was angry, unsettled, always thinking that the next marriage would make him happy. City records show Ralph moved a lot during Dick's childhood, changing rental houses every year or two, never able to buy a home or afford what everyone else in town seemed to have.

Lieutenant Roger Schmeltz, the police officer who was at the river when the body was towed to shore, had dealings with Ralph Kitchel. "We'd get a call that 'the boy is out of control.' Ralph was angry, shaken, because his own kid had defied him. 'He won't do what we tell him,' Ralph would say." Schmeltz would go to the house and find that father and son had exchanged fists. "In those days, there was nowhere to take a child, no foster care or resources." He would be responsible for talking them down and trying to broker peace before he left. After Dick's murder, Schmeltz would sometimes drop into the shoe repair store, but he and Ralph never spoke of the murder.

Schmeltz had taught mechanics in the air force but had other dreams. He moved to Corvallis to study forestry at OSU. His college education was interrupted by marriage. He was selling Fords and Chevys at O'Toole's on 9th Street when Ralph Kitchel came in one day. He almost sold him a car but Kitchel didn't like to negotiate and Schmeltz couldn't close the deal.

Schmeltz was looking for a career. He took the tests to join the fire department. While he waited to be hired, he continued to look at jobs. One day he was interviewing with a realtor when he was asked if he had ever thought of becoming a police officer. He hadn't. The realtor picked up the phone and called the police chief, and soon Schmeltz was hired. There was no police academy, so officers were trained by a sergeant they worked alongside on the night shift. He liked it. "I never wanted to be a detective, I liked patrols," he said. Corvallis was a small town with no home or business burglaries and very little serious crime. He liked knowing everyone in town. By the time of Dick's murder in 1967, Schmeltz had four daughters under the age of nine.

Montgomery and Hockema wanted Ralph and Sylvia to each take a polygraph. They had been driving a number of Dick's friends and the young men at the party to the Eugene Police Department, which conducted the exams. About two weeks after Dick was found in the river, Montgomery and Hockema told Ralph and Sylvia that an appointment for a polygraph had been made for them in Eugene. It would be at 7 p.m. in the evening, so it would not interfere with their business.

Ralph's first reaction was, "Oh, I don't know. I've got so much work to do around here." He and Sylvia discussed it, then Ralph told the detectives, "Oh hell, I guess to keep from being suspects, we'll have to get this thing over with." Arrangements were made for Montgomery to pick them up at their house to drive them to Eugene. That afternoon, Sylvia called them. They had talked with an attorney and he had advised them against taking the polygraph test "at this time." Montgomery shared the news with Knight and Police Chief Goodman. The men suggested the detectives find out who the Kitchels' attorney was. Montgomery paid a visit to Ralph at the store – conveniently when Sylvia had stepped out. Ralph seemed angry and said they would have to talk to Sylvia about the change in plans. They returned to the store when she was there. "She did most of the talking, stating they would be willing to take the test if their attorney was present," according to Montgomery's notes. That was only one of a long list of conditions she had. She interrupted the detectives and said, "I know my rights, and no one is going to force us to take these tests." She reminded them, again, that, "Let's face it, the high school kids hate you city cops and they won't tell you guys anything, but they would the sheriff's office, because they like them." Montgomery told her that if a student or any other person would rather talk to a different agency that was okay with the Corvallis Police Department.

The Kitchels had hired Ralph Wyckoff Jr., a prominent Salem attorney. Once Frank Knight had the name, he phoned Wyckoff. Both were respected, both would go on to be judges. Both knew about difficult suspects and clients. Wyckoff told the DA that he had no objection to his clients taking a polygraph, but he would like to see the results. The detectives notified Ralph and Sylvia that their attorney had given the go ahead.

Ralph didn't take the news well. "Okay, I'll take that damn test for once and for all and get you off my back," he said, according to Montgomery's notes. "I'm tired of being accused of this crime, and after the test, maybe you'll start looking in the right direction and leave us alone, because we didn't have anything to do with Dick's death."

Montgomery and Hockema followed their routine of talking to the polygraph examiner before a test was administered. It was common for the police to suggest questions that should be asked. The examiner spent considerably more time talking with Sylvia — before, during, and after the exam — than they did with her husband. She may have been easier to communicate with than Ralph was.

The detectives preferred to drive suspects to Eugene for the exam in a police car. It gave them a chance to chat before and after the polygraph. That didn't happen this time. The Kitchels weren't about to ride along with the police. They would drive themselves, thank you very much.

THE FUNERAL

Dick's friends stood awkwardly just inside the chapel doors at McHenry Funeral Home. Some were in sports jackets, some wore long sleeved shirts and a borrowed tie. For most, it was the first funeral they had attended.

Bob Wadlow, who had given Dick a ride to the party, was there with other members of The Patriots, his band composed of boys who had known each other since junior high school and having success around the Pacific Northwest. The main topic of discussion was about the casket. Would it be open at the service? They were more than a little nervous and excited about the possibility.

Six of Dick's friends were pallbearers, including Dean Beaudreau, who had an ability to see the best in Dick. He still does. Yes, Dick drank, but "not any more than any of us did," he said later. "He got along with everyone, and was friendly. He always strived to be better than where he came from." Dean knew exactly where Dick came from. "It was bad at his house. His dad was a bully and a drunk. Dick did not have a normal childhood. He raised himself." Dick didn't go into details about his fights with his father, but as Dean would say later, "*Someone* was hitting him." Despite the unhappiness at home – and the fact that Dick must have wondered where exactly home was – he liked to keep his room neat. Dick struggled in school, but that could be blamed on his parents. "I think he would have done well if he had had a good life," Dean said. By age seventeen, Dick had moved more than once between Corvallis and where his mother lived in Washington. He had two stepmothers, numerous stepfathers, at least two stepbrothers, and lived in a series of rental houses in Corvallis. His home became wherever his bedroom was at the time. His friends were his family.

Dick's funeral was held in the chapel at McHenry Funeral Home on NW. 5th, just two blocks north of Kitchel's Shoe Repair, at 1:30 p.m. on Tuesday, October 24, 1967. Judy Appelman, the cheerleader Dick would visit at her home and sit and talk with, doesn't remember why but her parents didn't want her to go to the funeral and refused to drive her. So she went with a girlfriend. It was raining hard. There were huge puddles and the chapel was crowded with wet coats, umbrellas, and people. Judy noticed that Ralph Kitchel was not wearing a suit and she wondered if he perhaps didn't own one. She may have gone to the burial in Albany because she remembers soggy grass.

Pastor Norbert G.A. Heins, a Lutheran minister, conducted the service. Organist Robert Eggers played the hymns "My Faith Looks Up to Thee," "Children of the Heavenly Father," "All Hail the Power of Jesus Name," and "My Hope is Built on Nothing Less." Ralph Kitchel paid $343 for the casket, and what McHenry called "other services" of $357. The minister was paid $20, and the organist earned $7.50. The body was not embalmed. It had been so ravaged by the Willamette River that there was no point. Dick's friends were relieved, and a little disappointed, that the casket was closed.

Out of respect for Ralph Kitchel and the fact he was burying his only child, the district attorney and detectives decided not to attend the funeral. They knew that, in his grief, Kitchel was directing his anger at them and there would be other opportunities to talk with him.

In what now seems like a supreme sign of optimism, given their combined marital history, Ralph and Sylvia bought three plots at Twin Oaks Memorial Gardens Cemetery in Albany. Dick was buried in the plot on the far right, a few feet to the north of the other two.

On the same day as the funeral, the news story, most likely written by Mike Bradley, appeared in the *Gazette-Times*. Lie Detectors Prove Truth of Witnesses, the headline read. Information attributed to DA Frank Knight said that three people who had been among the last to see Dick Kitchel – Paul Everts, Doug Hamblin, and Marty Tucker – had voluntarily taken lie detector tests in Eugene. "It appears they are being truthful to police," Knight was quoted as saying. Knight knew the results were not that clear cut. He had information he did not share with Bradley. It would not be the last time.

THE LAST ONE TO
SEE HIM ALIVE #1

Hockema tried the exterior door handle on the passenger side of the DeSoto. It was, as its owner had claimed, broken and wouldn't open. A passenger in the front seat would have to wait for the driver to exit the car before he could slide across the bench seat and out. Hockema opened the broken door from inside and walked around the car, looking closely at the front and back seats and the floor of the early 1950s four-door automobile. There seemed no hope of finding any blood stains or evidence of a fight. Like Doug Hamblin's hands, which had had time to heal, there had been plenty of time for its owner to clean the car. Hockema didn't think it was worth seizing the car and taking it to the police station for a more thorough inspection. It was disappointing that there seemed to be no evidence in the car, but the detectives were already focusing on two men: the owner of the car, Doug, and Ralph Kitchel, Dick's father. It is a truism in police investigations that the last person *known* to have seen someone alive is most likely responsible for their murder. Solving the case depended on answering one question: Did Dick make it home the night of October 11 or not?

Within two days of the body being found in the river, Detectives Hockema and Montgomery had taken the first of many trips to Eugene, driving Dick's family and friends to undergo polygraphs. Paul Everts, Doug, and Marty must have been relieved to see that, according to the *Gazette-Times,* they had been deemed "truthful." It was right there in black and white in the *G-T.* Truthful. Doug's polygraph was a bit more complicated. The Eugene Police Department's polygraph examiner, Sergeant G.E. Mitchell, wrote of Doug that "he is a seemingly calm, truthful, young man ... he wants to be of any possible assistance to the police in determining who caused the victim's death." Over two hours, Doug was asked if he had told the complete truth, if he had deliberately lied to the police, if he was concealing information, if he had a fight or argument with the victim, if he had choked Dick, and if he knew who threw Dick's body into the river. After the test, Mitchell concluded, "It is not possible at this time to render an opinion, and the results of this examination are, at this point, considered inconclusive." Before Doug left the examination room, he was told that they would like to do another polygraph. He agreed to it.

Montgomery and Hockema invited Doug to come to the police station to sit and talk with them. They tape recorded their conversation with him. He brought along Dick's jacket. They didn't believe for a minute that he hadn't known whose coat it was. He had rid himself of it as quickly as possible, handing it off to a boy in his neighborhood. But he had also admitted he had the jacket. The rest of his story seemed consistent with what he had told the detectives earlier about letting Dick off downtown. They decided to put a little pressure on him in hopes he might actually confess. He didn't, but he began to reveal more details and they were glad they were taping the interview. He admitted pulling on Dick to get him out of his car. The detectives had him demonstrate for them.

Doug stood and tried to mime how he leaned into the car to reach Dick. Instead of grabbing Dick's collar or his arm and pulling, Doug said he *may* have wrapped his arm around Dick's neck, catching the throat where his elbow bent. The detectives knew that fit with the autopsy results. They asked if his pulling on Dick escalated a fight between them. Doug said no. He insisted that Dick was alive when he drove off.

Montgomery, Hockema, and Knight were familiar with Doug's colorful family. His mother, Flo, was the daughter of vaudevillians and had grown up traveling from town to town with her parents. In Corvallis, she worked as a cab dispatcher and at Lipman's, the department store across the street from Safeway. The police thought of her as a "bar fly," although she didn't drink. She must have been an optimist because she was married eight times to six men. One of the police department's favorite stories involved her husband, Blackie, the father of Doug and his younger brother. Blackie had been arrested one too many times for drinking and driving and he had lost his license and car. So the next time he wanted to visit his favorite haunt, the Peacock Tavern on SW. 2nd Street, he drove his tractor to the bar and parked it nearby. A few hours later, he left the bar and on the way home, crashed the tractor and was charged again with a DUI. He hired one of the most prominent attorneys in town, Bob Ringo, went to trial, and was found not guilty. Blackie was a cook at Wagner's, the diner at 3rd and Madison, where friends and I drank cherry Cokes and I learned to salt the *ketchup,* not the fries.

Doug was well-known in town for being a wild child. He had quit high school before he graduated and married Teresa Marie Daily in Vancouver, Washington, on July 5, 1964. Their daughter was born almost exactly one year later. According to their 1966 divorce documents, Doug's wife claimed there was more wrong than the usual incompatibility. She said he was guilty of cruel and inhuman treatment and personal indignities toward her, for the purpose of "worrying, annoying and harassing" her, which was detrimental to her health and well-being. Hamblin was earning $400 to $450 a month at Finstad Heating and Sheet Metal. The court awarded $75 a month to Teresa. Within a year of the divorce, Hamblin's wages were being garnished by the Children's Services Division for non-payment. The police either didn't care or didn't know that when he was questioned about Dick, he had misrepresented his age, address, and other facts about himself, and had a reputation as a man capable of violence and picking fights. At some point after Dick's body was found and his initial questioning by police, Doug disappeared for a while, probably to stay with his father.

Just like his mother had remarried two of her ex-husbands, Doug and Teresa got back together, remarried, and divorced again. Doug was often in debt. One time he wrote a check to Fred's Honda to buy a motorcycle. He was long gone before the check bounced. It was difficult for businesses to sue him because he had nothing. He got into fights and scrapes, and had a reputation around town as a hot head.

Doug was close to his mother and often lived with her. His father spent some time in prison, and when he wasn't incarcerated, lived in Washington. Flo worked as a taxi dispatcher on the swing shift, and was not home a lot. Family members said that's why the boys ran wild. Martha Taylor, Doug's fourth wife, describes Flo as very short, under five feet, with a big bust and tiny legs and ankles. She liked to wear ballerina slippers. A photo shows her looking a bit like Judy Garland – round face with heavy eyebrows and dark hair. Martha had an idea about why Flo was who she was. She had lived an itinerant childhood because of the vaudeville life. "She wanted security, but she liked change. I think she was looking to have some sort of stability in her life, and I think the only place she found that was with Skipper, her first and her last husband. She didn't love him, but he was very, very kind to her and he loved her dearly. Skipper was very kind to Doug also."

Doug became his mother's protector. She was his protector too. When creditors called her house about his past-due bills, he might be sitting in the next room but she would say she had no idea where he was. Between his marriages, he sometimes slept in a small travel trailer in her back yard. "There was no one that cared about him like she did. He was basically a child emotionally," Martha said. Her two daughters by an earlier marriage disliked Doug. He was often angry, and his size, sometimes near 300 pounds, was intimidating. One remembers vividly the day he found her on the telephone and was so angry that he grappled with her for the phone and the cord became wrapped around her neck. Martha remembers a road rage incident during a trip to Hawaii. He had quit drinking before they married, but he could be mean and abusive.

Maybe it all stemmed from an incident in his early childhood when he lost the sight in his right eye. That, and moving back and forth between his divorced parents and often-married mother taught Doug a lesson he carried through his adult life, according to one relative: "Do unto others before they can do unto you."

THE WORN SIDE OF TOWN

Bernard Malamud called south Corvallis, where the Kitchels lived, the worn side of town. It was the end of town with farmland, trailer parks, and neighborhoods with small homes. It was where people who wanted a little space between them and the next house lived. The main road, SW. 3rd, also known as Pacific Highway West, or 99W., was lined with car repair shops, one of the town's first pizza parlors, and Avery Park and the troublesome bears. It was just south of the bridge over the Mary's River, near the confluence of the Mary's and the Willamette where the police believed Dick's body was dumped.

Malamud, who later won the Pulitzer Prize for *The Fixer,* moved to Corvallis in the 1950s to teach at what was then Oregon State College. He wrote several important American novels during his time in Corvallis, including *The Natural, The Assistant*, *The Magic Barrel*, and the semi-autobiographical *A New Life*, a satire of small town college life. Malamud called the town "Cascadia" and the Willamette River "Sacajawea" in *A New Life*. No one before or since has captured the stoicism of life in Corvallis. Sometime in the middle of the 20th century, the state had sent the liberal arts to the University of Oregon in Eugene. Oregon State College kept agriculture, engineering, and forestry. That fact played a role in Malamud's book. His main character, a writer called Levin, has left the East to teach literature at a college – except there are few literature courses and new faculty are stuck with composition classes. It was exactly what happened to Malamud.

A New Life was published just after Malamud left OSU in 1961 to teach at Bennington College and went on to win the Pulitzer Prize and National Book Award for *The Fixer.* The title of the book came from the name of a Corvallis handyman, Jim the Fix'r, whose store Malamud's writing office looked out on. I accompanied my father on many Saturdays to the shop. *A New Life* was met with disdain by Corvallis – Malamud seemed to be ridiculing the small-town life and campus. Corvallis greeted *A New Life* just like the fictional town in *Return to Peyton Place* did a local girl's expose of gossip and lust in her New England town. They were poor sports.

In the novel, the character of Levin has an affair with the lonely wife of his department chair. After the book's publication, one OSU English professor kept a sign on his door reading, It Wasn't My Wife. But the university eventually embraced Malamud and he was feted for his literary awards. In truth, he had made many friends in Corvallis. Many of our parents knew Malamud, just as some called Linus Pauling a friend. A 1922 graduate of OSC in chemical engineering, Pauling won the Nobel Prize in Chemistry in 1954 and the Nobel Peace Prize in 1962. Joseph McCarthy thought Pauling was being exploited by communist-front organizations. Pauling flatly denied being a communist. He *had* refused to comply with a subpoena in 1950 to appear before the California State Investigating Committee on Education and, like Harry Goheen, was opposed to loyalty oaths. As both Malamud and Pauling could attest, misfits were warmly accepted on campus *after* they won accolades.

If geography is destiny, where you lived in Corvallis – for example, in the worn part of town – was important. In the 1960s, well-off families lived on top of a small hill, where a golf course built in 1919 had become the Corvallis Country Club. Many of us lived in pretty neighborhoods near the campus. And there was everyone else – the farmers and small business owners, like Dick's father. As late as the 1960s, some homes skirting the town still had outhouses.

Tom Norton, who moved to Corvallis when he was in eighth grade from Stayton, twelve miles southeast of Salem, population about 3,000, thought Corvallis "looked like a movie set." It did and, in some respects, it still does. Downtown Corvallis is composed of stone and brick two-story buildings dating back to the 19th century. There is sprawl to the north and south, but the core downtown area reminds me of the towns in some of my favorite movies: *Pleasantville*, Hitchcock's *Shadow of a Doubt*, and Orson Welles' *The Stranger*. All feature towns pretty as a picture but with dark secrets.

The Kitchels lived in a modest house among other modest residences at 301 Bell Lane, about one mile from 4th and B where Doug said he had pulled over his car. By now, Detectives Montgomery and Hockema believed there was a strong possibility that *if* Doug had killed Dick, they had fought on the street corner and when Doug realized Dick was dead, he had put him back in the car and driven him to the low point where the rivers met just two blocks east.

South of town was where most of the grass seed farming was. Our close friends Margaret and Ken Coon farmed wheat, rye grass, and oats. I grew up with their three sons, riding horses and finding a close friend and a surrogate mother in Margaret. My friend Margret Murphy's parents had a dairy farm and grew wheat and rye grass. Margret's grandparents raised registered Suffolk sheep, chickens, and grew alfalfa on Kiger Island. Margret's father, Bud, eventually took over running Murphy's Tavern, his brother's place, a bar popular with college students on SW. 3rd. I met Margret when we were assigned seats alphabetically in eighth grade social studies. Dick Kitchel was two rows of students away. I sat in back of Margret and liked to tap her on the shoulder and bother her. She was shy, I wasn't, and I liked to make her laugh. I had met her twin, Alan, the year before. Like Sterling, they had been adopted, then her parents, like mine, had been surprised with a child.

South of town was also the site of a cult led by a con artist named F. Edmund Creffield. He was a native of Germany and was active in the Salvation Army in Portland. In 1903, he was sent to Corvallis on a mission. He soon broke with the Salvation Army, claimed that he was the second coming of Jesus, and started his own cult he called Bride of Christ Church, mostly all women he made sure were cut off from their loved ones. There was nudity and there was sex. In 1906, he was murdered in Portland by George Mitchell, the brother of one of the members. After Mitchell was acquitted of the killing, Mitchell was himself murdered by his sister in revenge. Creffield's dream of establishing a new Eden was over.

THE NEIGHBORS

The detectives went door to door in the Kitchel neighborhood in hopes someone had heard or seen something on October 11-12. Did Ralph Kitchel drive away late at night to pick up his son who was stuck downtown? Had someone arrived late at the Kitchel home? Any raised voices, slamming doors, or revved car engines?

The neighbors didn't have to be told there were problems at the Kitchel house. They had seen the police show up to settle fights between father and son. They knew Dick had crashed his car and been arrested for a DUI on Labor Day weekend. They knew Ralph could be easily angered. But no one had heard anything out of the ordinary. But what was out of the ordinary at the Kitchel home?

More than one person, during the investigation, implied Dick had it coming. There were wisecracks said to the detectives. The murder of Dick Kitchel, they said sarcastically, "couldn't happen to a nicer guy."

The detectives went to speak with Irene Kitchel, whom they described in their notes as Dick's ex-stepmother. She lived at 715 Wake Robin, just a few blocks west and on the other side of 99W. from the Kitchels. She worked at the Peacock Tavern. She said Dick had a drinking problem and that she did not think her ex-husband could have harmed Dick. She could add no names to a list of suspects Montgomery and Hockema were compiling.

The detectives must have talked to Dick's mother, Joan Borden, who lived in Olympia, Washington, where both sets of Dick's grandparents also lived. But there are no notes about their discussion with her. The police report does say that once Ralph told her Dick was missing, she had called the police department to ask about the investigation. She also phoned someone at the Peacock Tavern, maybe even Irene, to ask about checking the nearby waterfront. The Peacock was just two blocks from the Willamette.

Montgomery and Hockema went to the neighborhood near the employment office at 4th and B where Doug said Dick got out of his car. He said he last saw Dick walking south on 4th Street. If it was Doug that Dick had fought with on the last night of his life, maybe someone in that neighborhood heard or saw something. The area was a mix of small homes, apartment buildings, and businesses. The detectives spoke with the director of the Oregon State Employment office, on the very corner where Doug pulled over, who said he would talk to his employees and ask if anyone had found anything or noticed anything unusual one morning a few weeks before. They hadn't. The detectives looked around the street, but saw no blood or evidence there had been a fight. They did not hold out hope, since nearly two weeks had passed since Dick's death. They stopped at several small houses, but no one remembered hearing anything on the night in question.

Montgomery and Hockema continued to talk to Dick's friends. One said he saw two hitchhikers the night of October 11. Maybe the hitchhikers saw Dick, or had a confrontation with him. Police later located them but they had not seen Dick. One friend of Dick's told the police that Dick's father, before he finally went to the police to report his son missing, had called around to see if his friends had seen Dick. Another friend told police that Dick's stepbrother might carry a grudge because Dick bullied him.

One boy said he was at church on the evening Dick was at the party. He called Dick "a smart aleck," but said there were no problems between them. When they checked his alibi, it didn't hold up. They confronted him and he said he had mixed up his evenings. He was working at Albertson's market on Circle Drive that night, then had been at a girl's apartment with some other kids. His travels had taken him along the same streets where Dick may have been the last few minutes of his life, but he said he saw nothing. They also talked with an acquaintance of Dick's who knew him from Seaton's – who they made note was a "hippie type" – who told them everyone suspected Doug Hamblin of killing Dick. Montgomery and Hockema went to the jail where a seventeen-year-old runaway was being held. She had told authorities that she met Dick at the Everts' house in the summer of 1967. She had no information about his death and was just another young person who hung around with the Everts.

It was November 10, one day short of a month since Dick disappeared, when his father and stepmother drove themselves south to take polygraphs at the Eugene Police Department. The examiner, Sergeant G.E. Mitchell, always administered a three-phase test. As usual, there was a pre-test, before the subject was attached to the polygraph machine. It was followed by two sets of questions, asked twice, resulting in four charts. He not only looked at factors that might indicate lying, he tried to discern if a subject's answers matched what they had previously told the police. That's why the detectives always went early to talk to him before the testing began.

Ralph Kitchel's exam began at 7 p.m. According to Mitchell's report, Ralph right away launched into an explanation that he had high blood pressure and how it might affect the test. "Considerable discussion was had concerning his physical condition," Mitchell wrote. Mitchell did a short, preliminary test to determine if Ralph's blood pressure was within the acceptable limits for testing. It was. Then Ralph delayed the test with a discussion of what medication he was taking. In fact, the report acknowledges that the medication "has a tendency to dampen any responses in a galvanic skin response component of the testing process." Finally, the test began. Mitchell asked if Dick had arrived home (no), if Ralph had seen Dick on Oct 11-12 (no), if Ralph been truthful with the police (yes), if he knew who caused Dick's death (no), if he had caused Dick's death (no), if he knew who put Dick's body in the river (no), and if he had helped someone put Dick's body in the river (no).

Mitchell concluded that Ralph was nervous, but noted that nervousness does not indicate dishonesty: "It is the opinion of the examiner that this subject is not deceptive, and that the answers previously supplied to the police, and to the answers on this test, are the truth."

Mitchell spent time talking to Sylvia before beginning the test. "Mrs. Kitchell [sic] appeared to be able to speak much more freely of the matter," Mitchell wrote. "She does state that she has heard so many rumors that she does not really know what to think in regards to the circumstances of Dick Kitchel's death." She was finally hooked up at 10:17 p.m. She was asked the same questions as her husband, but in a different order and with "slightly different wording," according to the report. Her test ended at 10:55 p.m. Mitchell wrote that it was his opinion that Sylvia Kitchel was truthful. "Neither are responsible nor have any knowledge" of the murder, Mitchell wrote.

Ralph and Sylvia weren't happy spending six or more hours driving to and from Eugene and taking the polygraph exams, but now it was over. Montgomery and Hockema shared the reports with their attorney, as promised, and Ralph Wyckoff told them they had passed. Ralph hoped the police would not bother him until they solved his son's murder. He never, not once, called them to ask how the investigation was proceeding.

THE WIFE

When Detectives Hockema and Montgomery drove Paul and Juddi Everts, Doug Hamblin, and Marty Tucker to Eugene to take polygraphs, Juddi did not take the exam. They didn't consider her a suspect. Dick was, after all, beaten and strangled, then dragged or carried to the Willamette River. They *did* think that she knew more than she had said about what happened at the party at her house October 11. They needed to talk to her alone, without her husband present.

Juddi and Paul's connection to Dick was Juddi's sister Dawn. Dawn met Dick at Western View Junior High. They shared a desire to get out of their respective houses. "We talked about how miserable our lives were. He didn't like going home. He never felt welcome there, he felt in the way."

Juddi and Paul's house was a refuge for Dick and others. Yes, they could get alcohol. Juddi was a bit of a mother hen and the group of teenagers and young men in their twenties liked to hang out there. Paul and Juddi knew Doug from when Paul sold car parts to drag racers. But as the detectives discovered, just how well any of the key people in the Kitchel murder investigation knew one another was open to wildly individual interpretation.

There were inconsistencies in the stories. Paul said Dick was "a friend of Dawn's. He came over to the house once." According to the Everts' babysitter, Pat Hockett, Dick often stayed at the house. Paul said he didn't know Doug well. But Doug also spent a lot of time at the Everts', both before and after Dick's murder. Doug and Paul told the police that there had been some sort of disagreement with Dick at the party, and Paul admitted pushing Dick up against a pillar on the front porch to talk to him. Paul gave Dick a fatherly talk about his various problems, including his pending court date for drunk driving, then let him go. Others at the party said there was a more serious confrontation.

On October 27, and again on October 30, the detectives went to Corvallis Sand and Gravel to talk with Juddi. She was an attractive young woman who wore her shoulder-length dark hair up in a French twist. She said their parties consisted of drinking beer and playing board games. No drugs or pot. She admitted that Paul had once come to the attention of the police. He had been arrested for loud and abusive language in a public place – essentially disturbing the peace. He had stepped out of their house on N. 14th to confront some college kids across the street who were being loud. An Officer Williamson had arrested Paul. His bail was $20. They asked her about others at the party on October 11. She mentioned Mike Nader, whom Pat Hockett considered her fiancé. He was employed as a house painter. He was at the party and remained there after Dick left. The detectives learned later that Pat and Mike had recently been arguing about Dick. Mike thought Dick had been making passes at Pat. Mike had disappeared after Dick's murder, and Juddi claimed she didn't know where he was.

A more sensitive issue for them to ask Juddi about was her own relationship with Doug. The detectives used leverage to get her to confide in them: her two-year-old daughter. They implied they could create a custody problem if Juddi didn't open up. She did. She admitted she had dated Doug. They knew Pat Hockett had too. The babysitter had been in Doug's car when he wrecked it several months before.

Juddi went through the events of October 11 again. After nearly everyone else at the party had left, Doug offered to take the three boys home. Johnny Carson was on television. She was sure it was near midnight, because Marty was good about making his curfew and he left in time to arrive home at midnight. Doug left with Marty, Mel, and Dick in his car. She said Doug returned to the house before the TV show was off the air.

If Doug had beaten Dick and put his body in the river, why did he return to the Everts' house? What did he, Paul, and Juddi talk about? Did they pick up the drinking game where they had left off? Did Doug tell them Dick wouldn't get out of the car and he had to drag him out? If Dick had fought his attacker – and he had - did Doug need to clean himself up or borrow a Band-Aid? Or maybe Doug went to his own apartment and cleaned up before returning to the Everts'. There was plenty of time. He'd still get back before Johnny Carson was off the air.

Some people remember details from decades before, some don't. Paul remembered that within a day or two, he heard Dick hadn't made it home. And he remembered people saying that Doug may have been mixed up in the murder. He doesn't remember either Dick or Doug spending a lot of time at his house, but they did. And he doesn't remember the police arriving at midnight on October 21 to tell them that Dick's body had been found and that he had been murdered. Why wasn't the group shocked when the detectives stopped by to tell them Dick had been found, and he had been murdered? It was the same cast of characters: Paul and Juddi, Doug and Mel. Did they already know? Paul doesn't remember talking with Doug or anyone else about the murder. "If he had confessed to me, I would have turned him in," he said years later.

PHOTOS

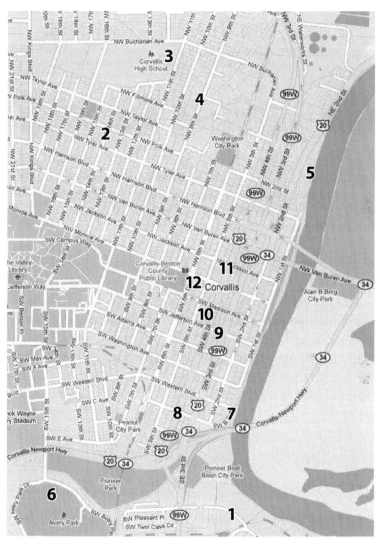

1. The Kitchel House
2. The Party House
3. Corvallis High School
4. Seaton's Barbecue
5. Riverview Marina
6. Avery Park
7. Confluence of Mary's River and Willamette River
8. 4th and B Street
9. The Gazette-Times
10. Kitchel's Shoe Repair
11. Benton County Courthouse
12. Corvallis Police Department

Corvallis Gazette-Times   CORVALLIS, OREGON   OCTOBER 23, 1967

Missing Prep Student Found Murdered

River Gives Up Strangled Body Of Richard Kitchel

By MIKE BRADLEY

The murder of a 17-year-old Corvallis high school student whose body was found floating in the Willamette river Saturday afternoon was under intense investigation today by Corvallis city police.

Richard M. Kitchel, son of Ralph M. Kitchel, 301 Bell Lane, a shoe repair man, was strangled, apparently following a fight in the early morning hours of Oct. 12, an autopsy indicated.

Frank Knight, Benton County district attorney, said the boy had been at a party at a Corvallis residence and had been driven to Fourth and B streets about 1:30 a.m. That was the last he is known

to have been seen alive, Knight said.

Argument At Party

The high school senior, who had been in trouble with police in the past and had drunk driving and hit and run charges pending against him, had been to a party at the Paul Everett home at 521 North 14th.

There had been an argu-

Corvallis Gazette-Times

CORVALLIS, OREGON
OCTOBER 23, 1967

Missing Prep Student Found Murdered

ment and a scuffle at the home, police said, and Doug Hamblin, 21, drove Kitchel to the State Employment office on South Fourth where he let Kitchel out of his car to walk home.

Others At Party

Others at the party were Mrs Everett, Marty Tucker, Mel Plemmons, 17, and a 19-year-old girl identified only as Pat, it was reported.

Those at the party have cooperated with police, Knight said, and have agreed to undergo lie detector tests at Salem.

The autopsy showed Kitchel had bruises about the mouth and eyes, and his knuckles were bruised, indicating he had been in a fight, Knight said.

Strangled, Autopsy Shows

He had been strangled, either by a person's arm or with the sleeve of a coat, Dr Russell Henry, state medical examiner who performed the autopsy Saturday evening, indicated. The boy was 5 feet 2 inches tall and weighed 125 pounds.

The body was clothed in the blue jeans and cowboy boots he was wearing when last seen. A missing sheepskin coat he had been

RICHARD KITCHEL

wearing was turned in to police Sunday night by Hamblin, police said.

Everett works on the survey crew at the Corvallis Sand and Gravel Co His wife is employed in the office there.

Funeral for Kitchel is scheduled for 1:30 p.m. Tuesday at the McHenry Funeral Home. (See obituary on Page 20).

Riverview Marina, lower left (photo courtesy Dan Eckles)

Dan Eckles, on the dock where a few years later he would spot a body in the Willamette River (photo courtesy Dan Eckles)

Kitchel's Shoe Repair (left) and Leading Floral

Corvallis High School

Avery Park bear pit (photo courtesy Mary Avery Garrison)

SEATON'S BARBEQUE PIT

Fast, Friendly Service

BARBEQUE PIT

Owned and operated by
Tom and Dorothy
Williamson

906 N. Ninth

PL 3-4827

Seaton's, the place to see and be seen

The Patriots – Left to right Darrell Selvig, Brent Durban, Dave Wilson, Rob Ford, Bob Wadlow, Roger Asbahr (photo courtesy Bob Wadlow)

Benton County Courthouse

Frank Knight, District Attorney

Corvallis Police Department

*Doug Hamblin and Martha Taylor on their
wedding day (photo courtesy Martha Taylor)*

James and Lucille Morris at the house on Western Avenue

Richard Nixon speaking at OSU, April 24, 1968

A SWEET SENDOFF at the tail end of the Oregon primary campaign was given Sen. Robert F. Kennedy as he made a late afternoon stop here Monday. The senator spoke briefly from the courthouse steps and was presented a jar of honey by Karen Peterson (wearing tiara), recently named Queen Bee by the state beekeepers. Miss Peterson, an Oregon State University coed, lives in the Dixie area of Linn county just east of Corvallis

Robert F. Kennedy on the courthouse steps, May 27, 1968

OBSERVING

Only recently have I realized that I've spent a good part of my life, and my career, thinking about people who disappear or die unexpectedly, how life can turn on a dime, and how families cope.

Ralph and Sylvia Kitchel coped with Dick's murder by going to work every day. Day in and day out, they were at the store from early morning to closing time. Evenings were spent drinking at the American Legion Hall or the Eagles Lodge, and bowling at the Moose Lodge. Ralph coped by being angry at the police. Detectives Montgomery and Hockema were on the receiving end of that. He must have been angry at Dick too. I can imagine him thinking and in his mind telling Dick, 'See what you've done now? The drinking, the partying, the staying away from home. You caused this.'

One way my friend Margret Murphy's parents coped was to keep Alan's wrecked car, the red coupe he was killed in, on a far northwest corner of their farm south of Corvallis. Margret says her pragmatic parents thought someone could use it for parts. But for years I looked at it from a distance, wondering what it meant that they would keep a visual reminder of their son's death. After many years, it was suddenly gone. Either it was towed or trees and shrubs finally obscured it.

I am an observer and an eavesdropper. Always was, and probably always will be. I ask too many questions, even of family and friends. I can't seem to turn down the volume on my curiosity.

It began with my mother. She told stories and I listened closely. She repeated them often, trying to make sense of the gaps in her life, until she died at age 97. Her father, handsome, roguish Harry Lester Sterling, had vanished around 1920, leaving her mother Mabel and five young children. My mother, Lucille, was the third of the five. She'd been born in the woods of Oregon in 1911 when Harry worked on the railroad. She was delivered by a Native American midwife, the first white child born in that area of Oregon — so the story went. She didn't have a birth certificate until she tried many decades later to get a passport. The family eventually moved to Corvallis; Harry worked at a dairy and one day he ran off with the daughter of the owner. A private detective hired by someone, probably the young woman's father, traced the couple to Omaha, where they had stolen a car. That was that, until sometime later when Harry wanted to return to the family. Mabel's sister talked her out of letting Harry come home, there was a divorce, and Mabel remarried a couple of times later in life. Many years later, my mother did what she could to track her father, but there was no record of him, maybe because those were the days before social security numbers. My mother said they never talked with their mother about their dad, out of fear of making her sad. His five children never saw him again, or heard from him.

It was a lot of work to cope with Harry gone, and whatever income he made. Mable, who would be industrious all her life, started a boarding house for college students. The family was so poor that at Christmastime, my mother and her brothers and sisters taped red cellophane paper to a wall and pretended it was a fireplace with stockings hung on it. When my mother was twenty or twenty-one, she met my father, who had finished his degree and was teaching physics at the college. He lived a block or two from the boarding house and had first seen her either riding a bicycle up the street or sitting on the porch of the boarding house. He was several years older, educated, settled, ambitious, kind, and loving. In some ways, Jimmie Morris was a father-figure. Both my parents grew up with uncertainty, which led them to look for stability. My maternal grandfather had left his family, and my paternal grandfather died when my dad was seven.

The other stories I heard repeatedly were about the heart-wrenching deaths of two young relatives who would have been my cousins but were born and died before my time. One story was about young Bobby. His mother, Mabel's sister Lena (the sister who had said good riddance to Harry) had traveled to Illinois to see their Aunt Ora. Bobby cried and begged to go with her, as if he had a premonition he would never see his mother again. But Lena told him he couldn't go, not this time. While she was away, she received a telegram telling her to hurry home. She assumed an elderly relative had died. It was only when she got back to Corvallis that she learned Bobby had chased a ball out into Monroe Street and had been hit and killed by a truck. The story was told in tandem with another one, about a boy who would have been my cousin Roger. My Aunt Dorothy and Uncle Ken lived near Dixon Creek. One day in 1944, Ken went looking for Roger, thinking he was with Dorothy. Dorothy thought the toddler was with Ken. To their horror, they found Roger face down in the creek, drowned. Years later, Ken walked out in the woods with a rifle and killed himself.

My mother's youngest brother, Jim, went down with his destroyer, the USS Barton, in World War II, just six months after the ship was commissioned. For the rest of her life, my mother couldn't walk on a beach and look at the ocean and not think of Jim. At about the same time Jim was lost at sea, her brother Harold was taken prisoner and spent time as a POW in Germany. All of this, except Ken's suicide, happened years before I was born. I never knew Bobby or Roger or many other members of the family, but I think about them. From them I learned that life can change in a moment. In my adult life, I would experience it more than once.

There were other stories that fed my interest in crime. When my mother's sister, Margaret, was seven years old she was a passenger on the train that became infamous for being America's last Old West-style train robbery. It was October 11, 1923, and Train 13, known as "the Gold Special" because it sometimes transported bullion and cash, was heading from Portland to San Francisco. The train slowed down to test its brakes on a mountainside south of Ashland, Oregon, in the Siskiyou Mountains and the three d'Autremont brothers, twenty-three-year-old twins Ray and Roy and their teenage brother, Hugh, boarded the train. They'd heard a rumor that $500,000 worth of gold was aboard. They'd stolen some dynamite from a construction site and were armed with pistols. They bungled it. They used too much dynamite to blast open the safe. It blew out windows up and down the train and sent smoke and fire throughout the cars. By the time the incident was over, the d'Autremonts had found no stash of money and killed four men, including the engineer. It was his last run before retirement.

The brothers hid in the woods and eventually adopted new identities. At the time, the search for them was the most extensive manhunt in US history. It took four years, but they were found and sentenced to life in prison. One was given a lobotomy. They were paroled in the mid-1980s and all died soon after. Unfortunately, Aunt Margaret was too young to remember the dramatic details.

On August 5, 1962, I was on a bus on the way to Camp Kilowan near Dallas, Oregon. That morning the news had been filled with reports that Marilyn Monroe had been found dead in her Los Angeles bungalow. My fellow Camp Fire members were busy singing "I'm Bringing Home a Baby Bumblebee" while I was turning over in my mind everything I had heard in the early reports, and wondering how I would survive a week with no news coverage. I had also followed the case two years before of William Tallman, who played Hamilton Burger on my favorite TV show, *Perry Mason.* He had been fired from the show in 1960 after police raided a private party and found nude or semi-nude guests with marijuana. The charges were dismissed by a judge, and after a letter-writing campaign by fans, Tallman was re-hired by CBS.

Locally what was making news was a lover's lane murder in Portland. Larry Peyton and Beverly Allan were nineteen-year-old sweethearts. On Saturday, November 26, 1960, two days after Thanksgiving, they were parking in Portland's Forest Park. Larry Peyton's body was found beside his car the next day. He'd been stabbed twenty-three times and his skull bashed in. Beverly Allan's body was found six weeks later in a ravine. She had been raped and strangled. Eight years later, three men were charged with the murders. Two of them were convicted and sentenced to life plus 25 years; one was paroled within three years, the other after seven. To this day there remains doubt about who committed the murders. My mother knew one of the detectives on the case. I don't know his name, or if he had grown up in Corvallis, but it gave her a connection to Oregon's most notorious crime at the time, so I had a vague connection too. Years later, my brother worked two summers at Crater Lake Lodge, where owner Ralph Peyton, Larry's father, hired many college students for jobs in and around the lodge. Larry and Beverly had met working there.

All of this time, I wrote. I always wrote. I kept lists – Mother said I learned that from my fourth grade teacher at Roosevelt, Mildred Stapleton. I wrote short stories. I wrote plays. I published a neighborhood newspaper and I wrote a column about the youth group for our church newsletter. I entered and sometimes won writing contests. My plays and stories had a reoccurring theme which I'm still pondering – a motherless girl raised in the African jungle by her scientist father. My dad would type up my stories. After submitting a story to *Jack and Jill* magazine, I received a polite rejection letter but was not disturbed by it. In fact, I was excited to tell my sixth grade teacher, Mr. Stevenson, but kept forgetting what the letter was called. I had to ask my father again. It was called a rejection letter. Even then, little could discourage me. My dad encouraged Sterling too, buying him his first record player and when my brother was two, sitting him on his lap so that his small fingers could reach the keys of an organ, and soon after, a piano. He began to play anything and everything by ear.

I don't remember reading coverage of Dick's murder, but I'm positive I did. My parents were newspaper readers and subscribed to both the *Gazette-Times* and *The Oregonian*. There were also a lot of books in the house. From a young age, I was reading what they were reading, including *In Cold Blood* and *The American Way of Death*. I remember vividly the news coverage of Richard Speck and his murder of eight student nurses in 1966. That same year, Charles Whitman killed his wife and mother, then took his hunting rifle and other weapons and entered a tower at the University of Texas at Austin. He killed seventeen people and wounded thirty-one others before he was killed by police.

I never thought I had a morbid curiosity. When I speak at libraries or book stores or writers conferences, I admit that I write books about people who do terrible things to each other. But I try and explain that the crime itself is the *end* of the story. I'm interested in what led up to the crime, what makes people the way they are, in what community the crime occurred, and how the crime affected that community.

I used to wonder why I didn't see my parents overtly mourn the deaths of their siblings or close friends. Now I understand how time takes care of that. As we experience loss year after year, the sorrow becomes familiar. Although I often saw my father with tears in his eyes, mostly when he was proud of Sterling and me, I only saw my mother cry once, shortly after I was widowed for the second time. I was only thirty-three. She said she would have changed places with me if she could.

Years before, I was walking down a hallway at Western View Junior High, on the way to home economics, which I was close to failing, when I heard that President Kennedy had been shot. I was doing poorly enough in home ec that my teacher, Mrs. Ballard, had the courage to tell my mother I was not doing well, either in the cooking or sewing portion of the class. The reason it took some courage, which I admired, was because her husband worked for my dad at KOAC.

I don't remember how my problems in home ec were resolved. All of us remember that day, and the weekend coverage of the assassination, Oswald's murder, and the funeral in Washington, DC. I had grown up seeing my father on TV and listening to him on radio, and being on the air myself when they needed children, so I may have had a different connection to the media than my classmates. I can't say for sure. I only know that from a very young age I understood and felt a part of the media and looked at it with a critical eye.

I wrote an essay once – but never tried to sell it – about how Jackie Kennedy did us a disservice. We are supposed to admire her self-discipline and how she contained her emotions after the president was assassinated. I wrote, knowing I was exaggerating and hoping that readers would know it, that I had more in common with Hindu widows who once upon a time were expected to wail at funerals and throw themselves on their husband's funeral pyre. The rite, called *Sati*, was rare and not really a part of Hinduism. But I could identify. I wanted this to be a world where it was okay to wail publicly because that's what I did privately. I grieved for twenty years before I had an insight that has brought me peace: Life is never, ever the same after a tragedy – which I define as an unexpected or uncommon death – but it can be good.

NOTHING NEW

Mike Bradley was stymied. District Attorney Frank Knight wouldn't tell Bradley much about the Kitchel case other than to say there was "nothing new," a phrase Bradley made a point of using in several stories; to readers, the cumulative effect suggested the police weren't aggressively investigating the murder. Knight had ordered the police not to share any information, so Bradley's daily visits to the police department and to Knight's office to pick up tidbits of information were for naught. Dick's murder was a big story in Corvallis and Bradley wanted to keep it in the public's mind. But how to do that when there was no news? He missed an opportunity when he never talked to Ralph Kitchel or Dick's friends to learn more about the victim.

For months, Bradley was relegated to writing stories for the *Gazette-Times* such as the one headlined Nothing New About Kitchel, published in late October. "Corvallis detectives are devoting full time to the investigation and are questioning many persons who knew the murdered youth," Knight was quoted as saying. "It could very well turn out to be a process of elimination in the questioning in trying to come up with someone who has a scrap of information we could use." There was little news in a statement like that. Which was the DA's point. Knight thought Bradley got excited and liked to elaborate on things.

A week after the most recent nothing new story, a story with no byline, most likely written by Bradley, appeared on November 4. The headline read Under New Setup – All Information in Kitchel Case Is Poured Through DA; Nothing New.

It's a curious story. The article points out how the district attorney and police departments of Corvallis and Salem handled murder cases differently. Bradley may have meant to needle Knight by explaining how much freer information was passed around Salem but he ultimately puts Knight in a respectful light. Bradley never gave up hoping Knight would admit the police were "baffled" by the case. In Corvallis, Knight controlled the release of information. "All information concerning police investigation into the murder of Richard M. Kitchel, 17, last month is being released only through the office of District Attorney Frank Knight," Bradley wrote.

The November 4, 1967, story is about a brouhaha at a Salem City Council meeting that pitted Marion County DA Gary Gortmaker against council members. Salem, our state capital, just 40 miles north of Corvallis, has always been about twice the population of Corvallis and has long held the designation of the state's third largest town, after Portland and Eugene. Although Salem is the seat of state government and home to Willamette University, a prestigious private university, it is also home to the Oregon State Penitentiary, Oregon State Hospital, where *One Flew Over the Cuckoo's Nest* was filmed, and other institutions. As a friend of mine who has lived there for years said, everyone in town is waiting for someone to be released. Corvallis never aspired to be Salem.

The ongoing controversy in Salem over the police sharing information with the press permitted Bradley to mention the Kitchel murder again. "The release of information to the press through the district attorney's office is in contrast to the procedure followed in Marion County," Bradley wrote, where the Salem Police Department released information to the press against Gortmaker's wishes.

Gortmaker was demanding the cooperation of the council and mayor. He had clashed before with Police Chief Benjamin H. Meyers, accusing him of obstructing justice and threatening him with a grand jury investigation. Gortmaker claimed Meyers was hurting the prosecution of criminal cases by giving the press information on suspects who had confessed, exactly what Frank Knight feared. City council members and the police chief weren't intimidated by Gortmaker, who was a steamroller compared to Knight, who was more subtle and more effective.

In the article, Knight defended his approach to controlling information by explaining he was worried about pre-trial publicity, as was Gortmaker, and protecting the rights of the accused. "I certainly have no objection to city and county police giving out information to the press. But it is the responsibility of all concerned that the rights of an accused person be protected.

"It's always a problem when pre-trial prejudicial publicity enters a case," Knight said. "In a case such as this (the Kitchel murder) when a trial could be the result, it is desirable that the district attorney be the source of information for the news media. An irresponsible press," Knight continued, "could use [information] in a way to defeat justice and disregard the rights of the accused."

A few years later, Gortmaker would know first-hand what it was like to be the accused. He was charged and convicted of several counts of theft and misconduct, served several years in prison, and lost his license to practice law.

Four days after Bradley's story contrasting the two counties, he had another story. Some Unsolved Murder Cases Remain On Books in Benton County was the headline November 8 in the *G-T.* "Is Benton County a haven for murder?" was the first sentence.

"Corvallis police have two unsolved murder cases on their hands, and a third has been dropped – written off as solved but unconvicted [sic]," Bradley wrote. He recapped the Kitchel murder and how Dick had been strangled, perhaps accidentally, during a fight and "his body thrown into the river in panic. But they have no clue yet as to the assailant – at least not enough to make an arrest."

The other unsolved murder was the death of twenty-seven-year-old Doris Snedeker, who was smothered with a pillow in her trailer in south Corvallis on December 23, 1963. Her death at first was attributed to a suicide. Two weeks later, the state crime laboratory reported that she had been murdered. "There were many suspects, including a key witness who was killed in a traffic accident shortly after the murder. Again, not enough evidence was gathered by police to charge anyone with the crime," Bradley wrote.

He could have simply stated that police had not charged anyone. Instead, what he wrote was more subtle and damning: *not enough evidence was gathered by police to charge anyone with the crime.* He was implying that the Kitchel and Snedeker murders had something in common: the police had not done their job.

The last paragraph heightened the fear Dick's family and friends had. The fact there were two unsolved murders on the books proved, Bradley wrote, "Corvallis and Benton County are not immune to violence – and that sometimes crime goes unpunished."

IN CASE YOU MISSED 1967

In December, there was an event that was either a lead to Dick's murder or a bizarre coincidence. On December 11, twenty-two-year-old Rondo Ernest Casey was found dead at the corner of 4th and B Street, where Doug had let Dick out of his car. Police determined that Casey had died in a fall from the roof of the state employment building. A story on December 13, headlined Police Eye Connection, reported that Casey's death was being investigated as a possible link to Dick's murder. On December 22, the *Gazette-Times* followed up and reported that Casey's death was accidental and was not connected to Dick. Casey left behind a phonograph record, which the *G-T* didn't name, and a gallon can of beer on the roof when he jumped or fell.

Tips and rumors concerning Dick's murder were still coming in. Someone said a band of gypsies had killed Dick. Others said that the family of one of the boys at the October 11 party had moved out of town quickly and mysteriously. There were rumors around school of a mafia or drug connection or that a gang from Albany had killed Dick. Maybe he was picked up by a passerby for sexual purposes. As often happens after a murder, a few unhappy wives called the police suggesting their spouse had been acting shifty.

It was obvious to Montgomery and Hockema that there was a feeling among Dick's classmates and parents, as well as the *Gazette-Times,* that they weren't doing enough. But they wanted to solve the case. They regularly begged Frank Knight to make an arrest.

The CHS class of 1968 was beginning its last few months of school. Some health classes held an assembly to watch a film titled *LSD – Insight or Insanity*, then listened to a panel discussion. The school newspaper mentioned a documentary that would air on national television on "the current situation of the Negro." It may or may not have been one of my articles for the *High-O-Scope,* the kind I liked to do on topical subjects, but the December 1 issue featured a handful of teachers and students discussing whether teachers had a right to object to a student's dress or hairstyle. The consensus was yes.

That fall, I met Jim, a year older and a freshman at OSU. On a blind date on November 11, we saw The Doors playing at Gill Coliseum on campus. I preferred The Beach Boys but Margret and I were soon taking scuba diving classes and fencing to impress him and other boys we met. Mostly we laughed our way through our endeavors. I wore the lime green dress and matching shoes to the CHS Christmas dance on December 21.

Another girl had already invited Tom Norton, so Alice Henderson didn't attend the dance. That didn't mean they weren't dating. They would go out one night every weekend, and the other night Tom got together to play cards with friends. In Alice's mind, they weren't really going steady so she dated other boys too.

It's common for newspapers to sum up the year. The *High-O-Scope* would wait until the following spring, nearer our graduation. But the *G-T* published a story, with Mike Bradley's byline, titled In Case You Missed 1967, Here's What Happened In City. It ran on December 30, 1967.

It began with two sentences that, as a journalist and educator, I would call overblown, over-reaching, and overly dramatic. Over the top too:

In Corvallis, the year 1967 was a year of concepts – ideas – thoughts. Some were carried out. Some died aborning. Some still lie smoldering, awaiting a breath to spring them to life.

As we face 1968, who can tell what new and strange concepts and ideas will affect our lives?

No one could question Bradley's commitment to Corvallis. Day in and day out, he was its conscience, always urging it to be better. It's hard to write the lead to a story aimed at taking the pulse of a town. Best to keep it simple, which Bradley did not. But the lengthy article, which ran nearly 4,000 words, did, as Bradley promised, "give a picture of life in the community," including "its joys and its sorrows, its gains and its losses."

He mentioned dozens of events, large and small. One drew the attention of television networks and magazines and newspapers around the world. Winter term, an anonymous student enrolled in OSU's Speech 113: Basic Persuasion and wore a large black cloth over his head and torso the entire winter term. His professor knew who he was, but the class did not. It was the kind of event that would quickly go viral in today's media environment. During the term, the students' attitudes toward "The Black Bag" reportedly changed from hostility to curiosity and finally to friendship. Bradley wrote, "While there were explanations offered, this experiment drew considerable skepticism, and, in the end, many still questioned the worthiness of the happening." In other campus news, Bradley noted that "most people took a dim view of the hippie movement among the younger generation." The university, though, thought its students were mature enough to change a longtime policy and let juniors live off campus.

The biggest football crowd ever at an OSU game watched as the Beavers beat USC, the number one team in the nation, 3-0 under Coach Dee Andros, whose nickname was The Great Pumpkin because he was rotund and wore a bright orange OSU jacket.

Bradley's year-end story said the town was thinking about a community college. There was a study of jail improvements. A third junior high school was under construction. The city agreed to sell 340 acres on top of Mary's Peak to the US Forest Service. Two deer at an enclave in Avery Park were wounded with arrows and had to be killed; a reward led to the capture of two young men. Nazi leader George Lincoln Rockwell came to the OSU campus "to peddle his hatred of Negroes, Jews and Communists," Bradley wrote. "He left the community shaking its head. And it was not too surprised when a few months later Rockwell was slain." Rotarians planted 57 trees around Jefferson and Wilson elementary schools. Fire destroyed the OSU dairy barn. The city proposed to change the name of 9th Street, but "the howl of pain from businesses along the street quickly killed the plan." The Moose and the Jaycees held their state conventions in Corvallis and both were considered highly successful. CHS graduated a record 519 students and OSU a record 2,464. The OSU chapter of Sigma Chi drew national attention and controversy with plans to admit a student of Japanese descent. One alum protested but Eugene Okino was finally initiated into the fraternity. John Thomas was named principal of Corvallis High School, then "startled" the community by resigning almost immediately after deciding he would rather continue teaching world history. Max McKinney became principal. The city council launched a campaign to install a sidewalk along every improved street in the city despite "bitter and vociferous opposition."

Bradley wrote that the year "brought close to home the realization that air and water pollution could threaten the way of life here." The American Can Company announced plans to build a pulp and paper mill 18 miles southeast of Corvallis, near Halsey. Although American Can promised to be a good neighbor, a meteorologist on campus predicted the town could expect about 150 "stinky" days a year. Civil Defense held an unannounced disaster drill to test the response of hospital personnel; a report concluded they were prepared. Bradley wrote that there were some happy male teachers at Western View Junior High when a former

Miss Oregon was hired to teach at the school. A tax levy on property in Corvallis reached a record $104.28 per $1,000 of assessed value. After the county said it would no longer fund the preservation of a covered bridge over the Mary's River south of Philomath, a campaign was launched to save the bridge. It was a dry summer and Corvallis was threatened with a water shortage. It hit 98 degrees on September 15, a record. California Governor Ronald Reagan and Oregon Governor Tom McCall rode horses in the Veterans Day parade at Albany. The boys on the third floor of Wilson Hall, an OSU dorm, got attention when they stayed under a shower for 14 days, setting a record. The first snow of the winter left an inch on December 18. Benton County turned 120 years old. City officials were "somewhat irked" when it was announced that officially there was no increase in the population of the city or the county in 1967.

Also among the thousands of words about the town, there was this: "Police were baffled when the body of Richard Kitchel, 17, was pulled from the Willamette River. He had been murdered about a week earlier, it was reported. It still remains as an unsolved case."

Mike Bradley finally got to use the adjective that irked Frank Knight. The DA never said it, but Bradley used it anyway. Baffled.

WINTER 1968

A YEAR UNLIKE ANY OTHER

The clock was ticking. As time passed, the odds of solving Dick Kitchel's murder lessened. Memories fade, people are less likely to come forward with information, life goes on. Montgomery and Hockema were pulled away to work on other cases. But they vowed to bring a suspect to Frank Knight who he could prosecute.

President Lyndon Johnson called 1968 "the nightmare year" because of the assassinations of Martin Luther King Jr. and Robert Kennedy, race riots following the killing of King, and protests against the war in Vietnam. In January, North Vietnamese troops attacked the US embassy in Saigon and dozens of provincial capitals and major cities in South Vietnam. The Living Room War brought images of carnage on both sides of the fighting into our homes via television. Demonstrations and unrest erupted on college campuses with demands for an immediate end to the war.

Not at OSU. Mark Goheen's father, Harry, had been dismissed from other campuses for his overt politics. Now he had tenure. He could speak up. The professor of mathematics held weekly antiwar vigils at the virtual heart of the campus, the Memorial Union quad, usually standing alone with a sign during his lunch hour. He wrote many letters to the *G-T* about race and Vietnam.

On April 8, four days after King was killed in Memphis, an estimated 1,200 OSU students, faculty, and townspeople marched from the college campus to the steps of the Benton County Courthouse. One sign read "We March In Support of King's Belief, Dream and Commitment." A photograph in the *G-T*, taken out a window from the top floor of the courthouse, showed the conclusion of the march with participants gathered on the lawn. Speakers included OSU President James Jensen, Professor of History Robert Jones, and one black student, Clayton Calhoun. Calhoun condemned the riots taking place in other cities. He said he wanted to be able to shout, as King had, 'Free at last – God all mighty [sic] – I'm free at last,' but told the crowd he worried that "the black man has no place in this society and no future to look forward to."

Goheen, who helped organize the march, also spoke. The *Gazette-Times* only reported the words of President Jensen and a few others. But his son Mark remembers how he broke down and cried when he heard of King's death. "It's one of my biggest regrets that I didn't attend the march," Mark said later. He was busy being a senior. "In my youthful silliness I saw it as a day off school. I didn't know ahead of time he was involved."

The people most affected by King's assassination didn't live in Corvallis or attend CHS. We had one African American in our class. After King's assassination, we did what other schools did and not much else. We held a clothes, toy, and canned goods drive and sent the proceeds to Willowbrook Job Corps in the Watts district of Los Angeles. Our class president, Bruce Nyden, personally delivered the collection to Watts and spoke at an assembly when he returned. He told us about the boarding house where twenty Job Corps boys lived, who could stay "if they keep drugs, liquor, and girls out of the house." On April 19, Donella wrote on the editorial page that King's death was "a setback for racial harmony and equality."

That winter, the ongoing issue that got the most space in the *High-O-Scope* was a dress code, hair length, and how much freedom other schools had. Donella and four other students spent a day at Albany Union High School. Albany had a closed campus, meaning students couldn't come and go on their lunch hour. We had it pretty good. We had an open campus and could leave in our cars and have lunch at Seaton's, or Bob's, or A&W. Albany students had lost their privileges after complaints of smoking by underage students, littering, fighting, destruction of property, and strangers loitering around the school. It fell to the teachers to enforce the new rules. "Teachers patrol the halls and parking lot during the lunch hours," Donella wrote. "The teachers we saw didn't seem to enjoy this." She wrote that while CHS had a reputation of being a haven for hippies, Albany students envied our freedom. In truth, we did have an informal dress code: no pants for girls, or jeans for boys or girls. My favorite sentence in Donella's wry writing after her day at Albany High was this: "The skirts we saw were short but didn't go to the extremes seen at CHS, and not one of us saw a girdle the whole day."

Donella's trip to Albany was prompted by the fact our student council was about to study the dress code issue and make a recommendation. At a critical meeting, Mark spoke up and asked why CHS students would *want* to give up the freedom of choice they currently had. The motion to form a committee to study a dress code failed and the matter was dropped.

Mark knew a thing or two about freedom of choice, the opportunities it brought but its potential consequences too. One of the tallest boys in the school, Mark was on the varsity basketball team as both a junior and senior. He loved being on the team. His father was not a sports fan; he attended only one of Mark's games, and sat and read a book during the game. Mark was surprised when his father left at halftime. Later when Mark asked him why, he replied that "all the players walked off the court and I thought it was over."

Mark had experienced anti-Semitism firsthand, even from his teachers. "The coach never liked me. I could never really figure out why. Was he an anti-Semite? I was too much of a non-conformist for him." The coach singled out Mark for the length of his hair. "He had a rule that our hair had to be less than one inch long. He actually measured it, and one time decided mine was too long." Mark went to a local barber who thought it was already short. He trimmed it, but not enough to pass the coach's test. Mark was benched in the next game. There may have been another reason Mark fell out of favor. "Toward the end of the senior year, I was hanging around with an 'unsavory' crowd, at least in his eyes. Coach heard rumors that I had attended parties where there was drinking. He used that as a reason to boot me off the team for 'breaking training.' I was heartbroken but there was nothing I could really do about it. So I didn't get a letter for that year."

The *High-O-Scope* reported that the student council wanted an uncensored bulletin board presumably to encourage unfettered feedback from students to the administration. Principal McKinney told the student council that it was a request that would have to be made to the school district. Then he bluntly told student council members that CHS students had a good thing going and if they thought their rights were being trampled on, it meant we had an exalted sense of what liberties are. With that, the idea was dropped for at least the rest of that meeting.

The irony of President Johnson's statement about Vietnam that winter that "peace will come … because America sent her sons to help secure it" grew over time. Members of our CHS class would die in the war and many of us would have our lives changed by it. Mine was. The outside world came a bit closer to Corvallis in 1968. We weren't old enough to vote, but we began to sit up and take notice. Oregon's presidential primary was important, and anyone who was anybody came to Corvallis after LBJ announced he would not run for re-election.

Dick began to occupy a distant corner of our minds. He was a part of our childhood, and that was ending.

THE LAST ONE TO
SEE HIM ALIVE #2

Detectives Montgomery and Hockema paid another visit to District Attorney Frank Knight. They wanted to discuss how to push Doug Hamblin. "We were hoping his conscience would make him confess," Montgomery said.

They were suspicious of Doug, chiefly because he appeared to be the last person to see Dick alive. Shortly after the murder, Doug had left town. They learned he had gone to Port Angeles, Washington, to visit his father. Maybe it meant nothing, but it could have meant that Doug was unsettled, worried after his first polygraph exam and dreading that he had agreed to a second one. But he had to come back to town eventually — he had a job and he was supposed to be paying child support. One of Doug's later wives, Martha Taylor, said he left town because of the heat the police placed on him. Word reached the detectives that Doug had started attending a church, Grant Avenue Baptist, and may have been baptized. The detectives planned to contact the minister to see if Doug had confided in him. It would be tricky, asking a minister to reveal what may have been said in confidence to him by a member of his congregation, but it was worth trying.

The detectives wanted Knight to take the case to a grand jury, but he didn't think it was time. "There just wasn't enough evidence there," he said later. "We would have run into double jeopardy." In the late 1960s, grand juries met only about once a month. In the case of a felony, the arrested individual had a right to a preliminary hearing during which the district attorney would present probable cause why the person should be held. Eventually, the grand jury would either dismiss or hand up an indictment. Now, there is often an adversarial preliminary hearing before a trial court judge, rather than a grand jury, to screen and determine whether there is evidence establishing probable cause and whether the defendant is required to go to trial and risk a conviction.

In the Kitchel investigation, "The issue wasn't winning over a grand jury," Knight explained later. "There was a saying, 'a grand jury would indict a ham sandwich if the DA wanted them to.' The issue was – was there enough for a successful prosecution?"

On November 1, the detectives drove Doug back to the Eugene Police Department for his second polygraph. It was the same examiner as before, Sergeant G.E. Mitchell. In his report, Mitchell wrote that prior to the exam he spent considerable time with Hockema and Montgomery talking about the results of Doug's first polygraph and what control questions to ask during the second one, including: had he become a Christian, and had he ever threatened to kill his stepfather? Doug's answers aren't given in Mitchell's report. During the regular part of the exam, some questions were slightly re-phrased from the previous test. Doug was asked: Was he responsible for the victim's death? Did he know how the victim died? Had he seen the victim's body put into the river? Did he know if the victim's death was accidental? Had he told the truth about how the victim left his car? Had he hit the victim? Had he deliberately lied to the Corvallis Police Department?

Mitchell wrote that he talked with Doug for about an hour after the test and told him it appeared he had been deceptive again. Doug maintained he'd been truthful. Mitchell asked "a final general set of questions, covering the particular items that subject maintained were bothering him, and the questions were formulated in such a manner as to specify those items the subject claimed were of particular concern to him." This isn't explained but it may have been another chance for Doug to attempt to answer questions where he was considered deceptive the first time.

Then Mitchell's report takes an unusual twist. "This subject is not deceptive in relation to the statements made regarding his knowledge of the death of the victim," he wrote, "however, it also appears that the subject has not been completely truthful in regard to some of his answers given on the control questions." That might mean that Doug was consistent in his answers about Dick's death, even if he was lying, but deceptive answering the control questions.

Does that mean Doug didn't answer yes, he considered himself a Christian? Did he answer no, that he had not threatened the life of a stepfather, and did that register as a lie? Control questions weren't random. Somehow the rumor about his threatening a stepfather had reached the police. Martha Taylor said she knew Doug hated one man in particular whom his mother had married. Maybe he had threatened the man and someone had told the detectives. No matter. The detectives would insist that Doug take yet another polygraph. The problem was, if he was their suspect, there was still no evidence to justify an arrest.

THE BOYS

His closest friends called him Dickie. Some still do.

Dick was happiest as a child. He loved summer baseball, riding bikes, and spending time with kids in his neighborhood. But his neighborhood kept changing. His father would move the family – Ralph, Dick, and Dick's latest stepmother – every year or so to another rental house. Or Ralph would send Dick to Olympia, where his mother lived. Our grade schools were important because they defined our world, both the parameters of our neighborhoods and our friendships. It determined which baseball team Dick was on and which Cub Scout troop he belonged to. *Belong* is the key word. Where did Dick belong? Dick's obituary mentioned he attended Franklin and Lincoln grade schools, but omits Harding. He may have passed through other Corvallis grade schools too. His father, who shared the information for his obituary in the *G-T*, apparently didn't know all the schools he had attended.

Dan Dickason grew up at 36th between Fillmore and Taylor, two doors down from where his friend Dickie lived when they attended Harding School. "Dick was friendly, seemed happy, smiled a lot," Dan said later. He remembers going to the Kitchel house and Dick pulling some out Playboy magazines, which must have belonged to Ralph, out from under a couch. A kind woman who was present – maybe Dick's mother, grandmother, or first stepmother – laughed along with the boys. She made sure Dick always looked clean and neat. Dick and Dan were in Scouts, except Dan's met at the Episcopal church and Dick's was based at Harding or one of the other grade schools. Dan's friendship with Dick changed when Dan's father, an entomologist at

OSU, took the family to Brazil for a year. Dan came back fluent in Portuguese and with the travel bug. He saw changes in Dick. "I could tell he was hanging around with a bad crowd." Dick's friends from childhood may or may not have known that he was often in fights or busy provoking others to fight.

The demarcation that would set in when we were teenagers – whose parents were at the university or were professionals, and whose weren't – didn't seem important when we were young. It became important and was another way in which Dick would feel excluded. Some fathers, like Dan's, left to do graduate work or to take a Fulbright scholarship. Where our fathers went, we went. Or our parents stayed after their education and excelled in Corvallis. When I was seven, my father somehow balanced managing KOAC, family, and church, and earned a PhD at OSU.

Mark Goheen also attended Harding with Dick. He liked Dickie and thought of him as "spunky." They played baseball together. But Dick's family moved to the other side of town and he and Mark went to different grade schools and different junior high schools. By high school, "we were stratified," Mark said. "We were separated by class, social levels, privilege, and status." Dan felt the class consciousness set in too. "We thought we were a cut above others, and that we were better than kids who lived in Albany or Sweet Home." It must have seemed impossible for Dick to believe he was better than anyone.

Jeff Almgren was in first or second grade with Dick, and in Cub Scouts with him. "He was a sweet kid. He earned badges for helping around the house, keeping his room clean, whittling." He remembers that they called him Little Dickie Kitchel because even then Dick was small for his age. He also remembers Dick's mother or a stepmother giving Dick time and attention. That ended when that marriage ended. Jeff has no memory of Ralph ever being at home when Dick was young.

Jeff's father was a carpenter and his mother was a substitute teacher. There was no money for him to have a car, and he did not drink. Jeff and his friends found Seaton's "a pretty tough place" and didn't go there much. Instead, they went to Bob's or one of the other hamburger places. By high school, Dick was "tougher, running with a different crowd, hanging out with auto shop kids when the rest of us were in college prep," Jeff said. Something else caused a shift in their social group. Jeff began skiing with friends. Dick was not a part of that, and would not have been able to afford ski equipment or lift tickets. It's hard to imagine Ralph spending the money so that Dick could join friends and learn a sport.

Bob Wadlow got acquainted with Dick when the Kitchels moved south of town. "I didn't associate much with the kids in town," Bob said. He had heard Dick described as "ornery, mischievous." Bob was busy with his band and had started to date Meredith Ramp, CHS class of 1968, whom he married the next year. Bob drove Dick to the party at the Everts' house on October 11 in his 1959 blue and white Plymouth Belvedere with wings. They didn't talk much, except about plans for Bob to pick him up later. He doesn't think Dick was drunk. When Bob returned to pick Dick up between 10:30 and 11 p.m., he was told Dick was having a good time and would get a ride later. Over the next few days, Bob noticed that Dick wasn't at school or around the neighborhood. Then he heard Dick's body had been found. "It was pretty traumatic," he said. He's always remembered the jacket Dick loved, his Pacific Trail with tan suede.

Dean Beaudreau knew Dick as well as anyone did. Dean had been born in Corvallis. His father was a chemistry professor at OSU. The family moved away but Dean was back for high school. "Dick knew everybody, he got along with everyone, was friendly and likeable," Dean said, "but he was hanging out with a rougher crowd." He doesn't think Dick drank any more than anyone else did. Sometimes Dean skipped school and went to Dick's house. Dick kept his room neat. "Ralph was a bully, a drunk. Dick raised himself. He was the original latchkey kid. Dick's life was going to school and doing homework. It was not a normal childhood." As Dick became a teenager, he was "real outgoing, friendly, he could mix with twenty-one year olds and cheerleaders." Doug Hamblin, Dean said, represented a rough, older crowd that Dick began spending time with. But he believed Dick had potential and remembers Dick as "always striving to be better than where he came from."

Dean was at school when he heard that Dick's body had been found and that his friend had been murdered. He needed to talk to someone, and went to a telephone to call his mother. Later, Dean heard a neighbor talking about the murder. He heard the neighbor say "good riddance," referring to Dick. Dean went to his bedroom and cried.

THE GIRLS

By the time Dick was a teenager, he had changed. The child who had been happy and sweet was angry. There seemed to be more troubling him that the usual teenage angst. His mother lived in another state. Stepmothers had come and gone. He disliked his stepbrother. Dick couldn't count on the one adult he should have been able to count on, Ralph Kitchel; in his father's eyes, Dick couldn't do anything right. The more Ralph tried to control him, the more Dick rebelled. He still had close friends, both boys and girls. But there was no more summer baseball or riding bikes in the neighborhood. In high school, many of us were in advanced classes prepping for college, while Dick took automotive and woodworking classes. We were splintering off into those who would go on academically and those who wouldn't. And it seemed to matter more if we were well-off or middle class or poor.

Girls were important to Dick, whether they had neighboring lockers, or he dated them, or they were pals. He had good, non-romantic friendships. He was decent. He accepted boundaries, when there were ones, like sitting and talking with Judy Appelman. He also overstepped them, evident in the DUI accident he had. I don't think he would have forgiven himself if Diana Eddins had been injured when he wrecked his Chevy.

The girl he may have been closest to was Juddi Everts' younger sister, Dawn. Juddi had escaped their household by getting pregnant and marrying during her senior year at CHS. Dawn got away too. In the fall of 1966, Dick lost his confidant when Dawn moved to California where her father lived. She married at seventeen, divorced at eighteen, and discovered what many others had: "when you run away, you go with you." She was living in Texas when she heard Dick was dead. She didn't have a phone but Juddi and Paul tracked her down and mailed her an article from the *Gazette-Times*.

"I'm not a crier, so I didn't cry," she said. But she was shocked. "I thought his dad must have been very angry" and killed him. She knew the best and worst about Dick. He was a loyal friend, but could be a belligerent drunk. More than one friend told the police that he never used marijuana, LSD, or any other drugs, just liquor. "He could get obnoxious, mouthy." Which fit with what her sister and brother-in-law told her about the October 11 party. They had asked Dick to leave because he was drunk. Paul could be a mean drunk too, and she knew the parties sometimes brought out the worst in people. The guests would give Paul and Juddi money, and they'd buy the beer. Juddi and Paul always hosted. "They had the party house, even as adults," Dawn said. "They switched from beer to wine" but little else changed over the years.

Juddi was nearly three years older than Dawn. "She was the big sister, and I was the little sister who knew nothing," Dawn said. "As adults, we became good friends." Over the years, Dawn, Juddi, and Paul talked very little about the murder. But she remembers Paul saying, "If it wasn't his dad, it was Doug Hamblin" who had killed Dick. Dawn always assumed Ralph Kitchel had killed his son during a fight.

Diana Eddins was amazed her parents let her go out with Dick. The rumors about him didn't reach her house until it was too late. Diana was passed over for rally squad – Judy Appelman made it – but Diana did the next best thing and joined the riot squad, formerly known as the pep squad, and got to wear a blue and white uniform on game days and shake pompoms. She was also in Future Business Leaders of America and fire squad. Margret Murphy and I also participated in fire squad, if you can call getting out of class to hold open a door participation. Still, as the yearbook stated, we "risked our lives making sure every Spartan had exited the building."

Other girls, like me, knew Dick from grade school and junior high, before activities and cliques separated us. As we became teenagers, it became more obvious that our families, and our lives, were different. "His parents were not important in town, and some people had more money than others," Donella remembers pragmatically. "He was a marginal kid, getting into trouble."

But you can never anticipate what memories stick with us. "He had the tightest peg pants ever," a classmate wrote recently on Facebook.

THE BABYSITTER

Pat Hockett proved to be elusive. Did she know who killed Dick? Was there a mystery to her comings and goings, or she was just another nineteen year old on her own trying to make a living?

The detectives learned early in the investigation that Pat lived at the Everts'. She watched over their two-year-old girl while they both worked. Pat also helped clean Seaton's after closing time. Pat is mentioned by first name only in Mike Bradley's story of October 23 as among "others at the party" on the night of October 11. She was, and she wasn't, at the party.

Montgomery and Hockema wanted to talk to Pat again and found her in Salem. Like other friends in Dick's life, Pat said he was like a brother to her. She told them that on October 11, she was at the house when the party began, but left to work at Seaton's from 11 p.m. to 1:30 a.m. When she got back to the Everts' house, Paul, Juddi, and Doug were alone, talking. The detectives were interested in any and all details because this was the time frame when Doug returned to the house after giving Dick a ride. But Pat's information was murky. In the detective's notes, they wrote that Pat said she didn't remember ever seeing Dick at the house. But then she told them that he often stayed there because of fights with his father. Pat was engaged to eighteen-year-old Mike Nader, who had attended the party and was at the house when Doug left to give the boys a ride home. She said Mike was either on leave or had been discharged from the US Army. He'd been staying with the Everts too, and might be in Corvallis or might be in New York. For a fiancée, Pat seemed to be a little uninformed of his whereabouts.

Over the next few days, the detectives heard a lot of gossip about Pat, Dick, Mike, and Doug. Dick and Mike had argued because Dick had flirted with Pat. Pat and Mike had fought too, over Dick's interest in her. When Dick was missing, Pat told a woman she worked with at Seaton's that Dick had been in a fight with Paul. To complicate things even more, Pat had dated Doug and had been a passenger in his car when he'd had an encounter with the police.

Hockema and Montgomery talked to a Mrs. Parker, who lived one house north of the Everts. Sometimes, with little warning, Pat would drop by with the baby and leave her with the neighbor. Mrs. Parker told the police Pat often used her phone too. Three days after police had met with Pat, she was back in Corvallis. She ran to Mrs. Parker's to leave the baby, saying she was going to look for a job. "But she was dressed in cut-offs and a torn blouse," not appropriate for a job interview if indeed she had one, according to Mrs. Parker. Later that day, the neighbor learned that Pat had moved out. Mrs. Parker shared a list of phone numbers with the police that Pat and Mike had called from her phone. The detectives kept checking with Paul and Juddi to see if they had heard from Pat or her fiancé. They had not. She had disappeared from Corvallis.

In early February, Montgomery flew to Garden Grove, California, where Pat had landed. She was working at a café in a shopping center. Montgomery was accompanied by Sergeant Beauchamp of the Garden Grove Police Department. Montgomery's notes are dated February 19, 1968, although Pat mistakenly dated her written statement January 19.

The girl had fled town and Montgomery was interested in why. "She got the hell out of town and I went to see if she was involved or knew something," Montgomery said.

They spoke for several hours. Pat told them that because of his poor relationship with his father, Dick spent a lot of time at the Everts'. She admitted she once had a romantic relationship with Doug but said they only petted. She mentioned two different cars driven by two different boys who had brought Dick to the party, neither of them Bob Wadlow. Both verbally and in a written statement, she described talking with Dick and encouraging him to get out of the car and come into the house. She said he seemed depressed and had been drinking but was not drunk. Dick told her he didn't feel like being around people, but she coaxed him inside. Pat left to go clean Seaton's. "I never saw Dick again," she wrote. When she returned, the only people present were Juddi and Paul and Doug. She asked where everyone was and was told there had been some trouble with Dick, and Doug had taken him and two others home. Doug later told Pat that he had been upset with Dick because of the way he spoke to Juddi and Paul, and that he had driven him downtown, let him out of the car, and driven away. She also told Montgomery that shortly after Dick had been found murdered, Doug had told her that he had had a scuffle with Dick and now was worried "the cops will be after him because he was the last person to be with him."

Dick's friends knew that the missing coat had been turned into the police by Doug. Mike Bradley had reported it. It made Pat suspicious. Dick would never take his coat off, she said, unless it was to fight. "Dick always was wearing his coat," she told Montgomery. "Why did he take it off that night?" The detectives knew this was important to the case. Dick had been in a fight after he had left the Everts'. Even after his body had been in the Willamette River for ten days, it was obvious he had been brutally beaten and strangled. The fact he'd taken off his coat and left it in Doug's car was damning.

Pat didn't remember if Doug looked beat up at all when she saw him back at the house early on the morning of the

12th. She told Montgomery that Doug had a violent temper, and she'd seen it for herself the night she was in his car and he'd been chased by the police.

As for her fiancé, she said Mike left Corvallis because the couple had fought. "I told him that I didn't want to marry him … he was too different and lazy and it just wouldn't work out."

Pat hadn't fled Corvallis over something she knew about the murder – she had simply been offered a steady job and took it. "I would have brought her back in a minute if she knew something," Montgomery said. "I always had a strong feeling she didn't know who had killed Dick, but she had a gut feeling it was Doug."

In her statement, Pat touched on why she had left town:

Before I left, I was questioned by the detectives at Corvallis. They told me that the baby of Paul and Juddi Everts could be taken away from them. It scared me and then when Juddi came home, I told her about it. They got very upset & said to shut up before I got them all in trouble. Because of the drinking that had gone on in there [sic] house. So I decided that since I was clear & I could prove where I was that I'd just leave before I lost the baby or got them more greif [sic].

Later that spring, a detective in the Garden City Police Department interviewed Mike. He was living in Anaheim. He said the group at the party was playing a drinking game and when Dick swore at Juddi, Paul took Dick out on the front porch.

When they came in Richard was crying and I'm pretty sure he apologized to Judy [sic]. I left the room at this time to stay out of their argument. They continued hasling [sic] each other for a while, while Judy [sic] was virtually begging Paul to drop it. If I was able to speak to Pat I could remember at lot more, I'm pretty shure [sic].

Apparently Mike and Pat did not get together to talk. There is no mention of either of them beyond their separate California interviews.

What was troubling Dick that night? No one was asked if they knew what was on his mind. If Pat and her fiancé were asked details about the fight on the Everts' porch, what it was about, and who the scuffle was between, there is no record of it. Different people told different stories. Marty Tucker said it was Paul Everts who held Dick by the front of his shirt and backed him up to the porch rail. Others said it was Doug.

Did Doug and Dick continue their fight when they were alone in the car? If there was a deadly fight and Doug put Dick's body in the river, how could the detectives and district attorney prove it? It would be incriminating if Doug had hidden the fact he had Dick's coat. He could have easily disposed of it, but he admitted finding it in his car and giving it to a neighbor child, then retrieved it for the police.

The investigation seemed, to quote Jim Montgomery, "dead in the water."

THE STEPBROTHER

Dick Kitchel had little use for his stepbrother, Roger Bicks. Dick's friends knew that he bullied Roger. Roger was a couple of years older than Dick and bigger, but Dick was on track to finish high school in a few months, and would probably get a job working with cars or tools. Once Dick graduated, got out of the house, and got a job, he would be okay. Maybe he would drink less when he wasn't so unhappy. "He wanted to be a good boy, he wanted to be a good person," Judy Appelman said. Dick fought terribly with his dad, but Dick and stepmom Sylvia seemed to have a bond. She gave him spending money and her own son was jealous of their relationship. "She seems to think a lot of him," Roger told the detectives.

Roger had a checkered past, more so than Dick. He'd been trouble at both CHS and at the high school in Cottage Grove, Oregon. An administrator at CHS told the police that Roger had a violent temper and had been expelled for non-attendance. He went so far as to say that he "was a borderline mental case," and that it was impossible for Dick and his stepbrother to exist in the same house. Roger had a police record in Cottage Grove for shoplifting, disturbing the peace, drunkenness, being a minor in possession, and pushing a reserve deputy around. School records showed he was "surly, lippy and smart aleck," didn't attempt to get along with students or teachers, and was "almost capable of doing anything."

Finally, thought Montgomery and Hockema, here was a true enemy of Dick's. But he had an alibi. Or did he? They first spoke with him at the Bell Lane house soon after

Dick's body was found. On another day, they dropped by unannounced. They waited while he dressed and took him down to the courthouse and talked to him in a grand jury room on the third floor. For most people, this would be intimidating. If Roger thought it was, he hid it behind anger. Like his mother, he boasted that "he knew what his rights were." In his case, he admitted his frequent encounters with the police were his education into his constitutional rights. The detectives told him he was no more a suspect than anyone else. Roger told them that he wanted to help find Dick's killer. He made light of his issues with Dick. He said he had no problems with him, but admitted they kidded around and made remarks to each other. They had never exchanged blows and he would be willing to take a polygraph.

He said that Dick and Ralph had frequent arguments and they often shouted at each other over Dick's drinking. His mother had told him that the two had had a fight that left both with black eyes.

Roger had been hunting in Cottage Grove on October 11, and called home to be picked up. A brother, who worked at Evans Products and also lived at 301 Bell Lane, drove to get him. Roger said they arrived back at the house at about 1 a.m. Ralph and Sylvia were watching TV. The four of them chatted for a while, then retired for the night. Montgomery and Hockema had checked his alibi and could find no evidence that he had been in Corvallis the evening of the party. But they played a kind of "what if" with him. Where in the river did he think the body might have been placed? He immediately said Mary's River, then a few moments later suggested a park along the Willamette.

They drove him to Eugene for a polygraph. The polygraph examiner, Mitchell, described Roger as a very slow talking, calm young man. After discussions with the Corvallis police, Mitchell spent a considerable period of time talking with Roger about his relationship with Dick.

Roger ranted about the small slights, the disagreements, the jealousy, and the role each had in their family. Mitchell wrote that during the pre-test interview, Roger told him that

The victim, when intoxicated, was quite obnoxious, and given to making statements which would lead to violent arguments and actions on the part of the persons hearing the statements. The subject related an instance wherein the victim had told him he was going to have intercourse with his (Bick's) girlfriend. However... when the victim sobered up, he apologized, not only to him but also to the girlfriend ...

He (Bicks) stated he did become irritated, at times, with the victim, and there were some occasions when they did argue, however he did not, at any time, ever become so infuriated with the victim that he wanted to do any bodily harm to him.

In addition to the information regarding his relationship with the victim, considerable period of time was spent in discussing his activities on the night of October 11 and the morning of the 12. Again, the subject maintains that he did not see the victim after he returned to the home from Cottage Grove.

Once the exam began, he was asked two sets of questions twice. Some questions were deliberately included to test what he had already told police, especially about not seeing Dick the night of the 11th. During the polygraph, Roger was asked if he had put Dick's body in the river (no), if he had seen Dick's body put in the river (no), if he saw his stepfather have a fight with Dick that night (no), and if Dick had come home on October 11 (no). The examiner wrote that particular care was spent examining the charts, probably because of the detective's suspicions, but that "there are no indications of deception present in the examination."

SPRING 1968

DUCK AND COVER

It was most likely during the Cuban Missile Crisis in October 1962 when my family devised a plan to reunite in the event of a nuclear attack. We would meet at our cabin at Odell Lake. Just how Sterling and I were to *get* there if we were separated from our parents wasn't clear. The cabin was a two and a half hour drive, first south to Eugene, then east with a steep climb up Highway 58 to the summit of the Cascades. I was twelve, and he was fifteen or sixteen, but it brought me solace, and still does, that we would somehow find each other. My parents sold the cabin in 1976, but it remains the place I would want to be when the world ended.

When we were children, we practiced duck and cover in our grade schools. We may have been shown the official Civil Defense Department film featuring Bert, an animated turtle, who, to a musical accompaniment, demonstrates ducking into his shell for protection from nuclear war. The 1951 film also features children practicing ducking under desks, cafeteria tables, or by the side of a road, and covering the back of their heads with their hands. The message, spoken over and over in the film, is that children will have to take care of themselves. There may be no adults around. The narrator says it more than once. In one creepy scene, a teenage-girl looks for help and a man on the street puts his arm around her to take her to a shelter. Today, students rehearse emergency plans for school shootings. Both used to seem improbable threats, although less improbable as time passes, and depend on survival plans that can't be tested, until they are.

Corvallis showed up on a *Scholastic Magazine* map as a likely nuclear target, in part because of Camp Adair, just nine miles north of town. Adair was used as a training facility for infantry divisions between 1942 and 1945. My father, who was too old to serve in the military, taught physics at Adair during the war, in addition to leading KOAC's programming and all that entailed, from livestock reports and news of the war to live radio plays. In 1955, the air force acquired Adair and it served as headquarters for the 26th Air Division North American Air Defense Command (NORAD), an anti-bomber defense system responsible for defending seven Western states. Hence Corvallis as a target.

It's laughable now that we thought school children would be safe if they hid under desks, the combo ones where the desktop is attached to the chair. Mark remembers that his father was naturally skeptical about our duck and cover preparation. Harry Goheen knew that if Adair was targeted by Russia, we would be vaporized in a direct attack and would not be around for lingering effects like radiation sickness. Our desks would not protect us.

The US government encouraged Americans to prepare and offered plans called "family shelter designs." There were eight types, with names like Basement Sand-Filled Lumber Lean-To Shelter, and Outside Semi-Mounded Steel Igloo Shelter. The designs came with detailed instructions, a list of supplies required, and a price estimate – most cost around $75 to build, a small price to pay for the life of a family and protection from aliens, nuclear warheads, or from ourselves.

I was scared to death, thanks to the *Twilight Zone* episode "The Shelter" (season 3, episode 3, which aired in 1961), about an impending nuclear attack and a neighborhood turning on the one family with the foresight to build a bomb shelter. Mark's sleep was disturbed by a different *Twilight Zone* episode, "The Monsters Are Due on Main Street" (season 1, episode 22), about the paranoia that infects a neighborhood when there is suddenly no electricity. At the end, we learn that the crew of an alien spaceship is nearby with plans to conquer Earth, one neighborhood, one power outage at a time.

In 1961, President Kennedy had encouraged every citizen to build a fallout shelter. Friends of my parents lived on the hill near the country club. One Christmas we were given a tour of their basement fallout shelter, stocked to the ceiling with canned food. There were probably more bomb shelters around Corvallis than anyone knew. Some were in basements, but others were above ground and looked like small concrete bunkers. Years later, homeowners were faced with disguising their bunker or somehow getting rid of it if they wanted to sell their home.

In 1960, the university added a fallout shelter in the basement of Gill Coliseum, the athletic facility where OSU played basketball, where KOAC had put its TV studio, and the home of the Horner Museum. The prominent feature in the shelter was a large drum. On the outside, it listed its contents, including medicine and toilet paper. The inside was designed to be used as a toilet.

By the time we were seniors, there were no more duck and cover exercises. Adair closed in 1969 and Oregon's second-largest town of 50,000 — nearly twice the size of Corvallis during Adair's heyday — was abandoned. But the Cold War was still with us and Corvallis hadn't given up on civil defense preparedness. In 1968, a letter and a map were mailed out to all of Corvallis. Addressed to "Citizens of Benton County," it included information on local fallout shelters. Another pamphlet was titled "Protecting Your Family and Livestock from Nuclear Fallout." The advice was the more livestock the better; if crowded into a barn, they would protect each other. Stores of clean food and water should be set by. Good luck with your farmland; radiation will contaminate crops.

The town was divided into zones with air raid sirens and shelters. Occupants of every home were alerted to which shelter to head for. There were dozens of places, including campus dorms, the Benton Hotel, bank buildings, the Safeway near Kitchel's Shoe Repair, the post office, and the water treatment plant. Our house, at 1850 Western Avenue, fell into Grid #17. We were instructed to go to one of four nearby campus dorms.

I imagine that by 1968, this information got tossed or stuffed in drawers all over Corvallis, as I assume it did at our house. Russia didn't seem as threatening as the streets or campuses across America, or the country where we were sending our young men to fight.

Maybe we've returned to the days of preparing for the worst? Sales of do-it-yourself fallout shelters in America increased 700 percent after the election in November 2016.

THE LAST ONE TO
SEE HIM ALIVE #3

In March, Montgomery and Hockema met Doug at the Department of State Police in Salem. They thought the polygraphs conducted at the Eugene Police Department were credible, but wanted to know what a different examiner might conclude. Doug had someone with him for moral support. The minister of the church he was attending accompanied him.

The report, by Corporal E.E. Teuscher of the State Police, was much briefer than the other two polygraph reports.

Issue: The victim Richard Kitchel attended a party the night of 10-11-67 and 10-12-67. He was given a ride by Douglas Hamblin when he left the party. His body was found in the Willamette River 10-21-67.

Opinion: Definite deceptive reactions are found to relevant questions. It is the examiner's opinion that the subject is definitely withholding information and is probably responsible for the victim's death.

There it was, finally. Doug Hamblin was *probably responsible* for the victim's death.

The detectives and DA Frank Knight could not rejoice. The report definitely narrowed their list of suspects, but the results were not admissible in court. No one else had inconclusive or false polygraphs and there was no physical evidence that Doug had killed Dick.

They had examined Doug's car – nearly two weeks after Dick had ridden in it. There was nothing that showed a badly injured or dead boy had been in it. There was time in Doug's schedule that night that could not be accounted for. If Doug left the party in time to get Marty home before his midnight curfew, what was he doing for the next ninety minutes? Driving Mel home and Dick downtown might have taken twenty minutes tops. Where had more than an hour gone? Did he go to his apartment and clean up before he returned to the Everts' house?

Montgomery and Hockema thought they knew. Doug had pulled Dick out of his car, as he had demonstrated in their office, and then a fight broke out. Dick must have stopped to take off his coat, and put it in the car where he thought it would be safe. There had been a horrible fight and Doug found himself with a dead body. He must have put Dick in the car and driven a couple of blocks east, to a low point on the bank near where the Willamette and Mary's River meet. There was a trail of sorts and he would have carried or dragged Dick to that spot and dumped his body into the water. Or Doug had never stopped at 4th and B Street to let Dick out. Maybe they argued in the car and Doug drove to an out-of-the-way spot, near the two rivers, to fight it out with Dick. When he saw that Dick was dead, it would have been just a few feet to the confluence of the rivers.

Eventually, Doug drove *back* to the Everts' house. He either did or didn't speak to Paul and Juddi about what had happened. After the third polygraph, Doug's attorney told Frank Knight to either arrest him or back off. Montgomery and Hockema urged Knight to charge Doug. But Knight would tell them, "not enough, there's not enough."

Montgomery and Hockema went to speak with the man who had become Doug's minister. Although he was not a Catholic priest, the Baptist minister was still confined by a moral obligation to maintain confidentiality. The clergy-penitent privilege is the legal mechanism that prevents clergy or counselors from being required to disclose confidential communications in a court proceeding. It's designed to protect the accused, not the clergy. In 1999, Oregon adopted a bill that gives clergy members the same type of immunity long granted to spouses, whose conversations are privilege. But in 1968, this was an area open to interpretation. When the detectives spoke to Doug's minister, he shared a confidence. "He told us, 'If you are looking at Doug Hamblin, you are looking in the right direction,'" Jim Montgomery said.

For the rest of his life, Doug was troubled. Was it losing the sight in one eye when he was a child? Was it because his father was largely absent, and his beloved mother was busy with her eight marriages? Did his part in Dick's death affect him so that he made troubling choices the rest of his life?

Martha Taylor met Doug when she was a waitress at The Big O in 1974. When Alice Henderson worked at The Big O right after high school, she was one of the carhops on roller skates. The gimmick was wildly popular in Corvallis, but part of the attraction was trying to trip them up. People would deliberately leave their chewed gum in a spot that might stop a skate in its tracks and trip up a waitress balancing a tray of food.

The waitresses weren't wearing roller skates by the time Martha worked there. Doug would stop by, buy a 15 cent Coke and tip her $1. She thought it was his way of flirting. Then he'd take a job in Alaska and be gone for a while. Their first date was at the town's first Chinese restaurant, the Toa Yuen, on 9th Street. Martha's two children and Doug's mother went along. Later, Martha discovered he had a terrible reputation in town. "He didn't pay his bills, he declared bankruptcy two years after we married." Sometimes he worked with his brother as a hunting and fishing guide. He was a natural born salesman and over the years worked at a gun shop in Philomath, built boat trailers, was a long-haul truck driver, a private pilot, bought and sold airplane parts, chopped and hauled wood, and logged in Alaska. Family members, except for his mother, distanced themselves from him because of his problems. "He had a lot of scrapes in his life," Martha said. Doug was a risk taker, sailing alone in storms and walking away from the crash of a plane in a field in Idaho. He had affairs. He lied. He used his friends.

He never got over his mother's death in 1986. "Doug was never the same after she died. There was no one that cared about him like she did. He was basically a child emotionally," Martha said. Even when Flo was still alive, he was always looking for another mother. "He wanted that from me, but I had two kids to raise; I needed him to be a man and help me raise them. He just didn't have that in him."

Martha stayed married to Doug for almost fifteen years. The most he told her about being a murder suspect was, "They never charged me." But Martha believes that something happened. "He told me his version – there was some kid, he was the last person to see him, he had been accused of murder but never charged." Saying 'they never charged me' is not exactly a confession, nor a defense that he was innocent.

Over the years, Martha decided that it must have been an accident. Doug and Dick argued, Doug grabbed Dick, and something went terribly wrong. "Doug was really, really strong, physically."

The two went to marriage counseling. The counselor told Martha in private that Doug had told him something important about his past – but the counselor could not tell Martha what that was. Had he admitted the murder not only to a minister, but to a counselor, another professional sworn to secrecy?

At some point during her marriage to Doug, Martha went to see an attorney over a child custody case involving her first husband, the father of her two daughters. The attorney studied some paperwork, looked up at her and said, "Oh, you're married to Doug Hamblin, the only man in Corvallis to get away with murder."

WESTERN AVENUE

When I can't sleep, I imagine walking through our house at 1850 Western Avenue, the home my parents built in the 1930s. I thought it was the most beautiful home in town, with its white picket garden gate, pink dogwood, and various patios. There is a photo of my parents taken in 1942, leaning on the gate, flirting with each other. The house is gone now – just an empty plot of land the university wanted badly enough in 1968 to buy or condemn along with others so it could build more dorms. The pink dogwood was left and held out for years, then it was gone too.

I was born late in life to parents who were educated, settled, successful, cheerful and fun-loving. They didn't drink, smoke, yell, swear at or hurt each other. They were active in a church. I often saw them hold hands. They must have wondered what planet Sterling and I came from because we frequently fought. I've wondered if a factor in our sibling rivalry might have been that we were *both* the first-born. But I often say that adopting Sterling is the best thing my parents ever did for me. It's true.

My parents, Jimmie and Lucille Morris, were not goody-two-shoes or prudish. They hosted raucous parties with games like "Give me something you didn't wear to bed last night," which prompted hearty laughter when people got down to their last earring or shoe. It never went further. Another game involved passing an orange from under your chin to someone else's chin. I see on Google that this remains a party game, the Orange Chin Relay Race. Guests are divided into two teams. Each player passes an orange down the line using only their chins, no hands allowed! If it's dropped, that team continues with the person who last passed it successfully. The first team to get to the end of their line wins. Instructions say a ball can work in a fix, but it is not nearly as much fun as an orange or a water balloon. I am lucky, and I know it, that the strongest memory I have of my parents is laughter.

My father had become fascinated with the wireless as a teenager in Eugene. The stories about early radio tuners made from Quaker Oats boxes are real. He began building and selling them, moving on to wood and metal after cereal boxes. He was first associated with KOAC radio in 1924 when he was an electrical engineering student at OAC. In 1928, he was a physics instructor and began working as a remote control operator on broadcasts. Over the years, he became program manager, then manager, of KOAC and its television off-shoot KOAC-TV, and a pioneer in what grew to be public broadcasting (NPR and PBS). During his nearly forty years at KOAC, he called OSU and UO basketball and football games, wrote and produced radio plays, worked with live orchestras, read the news, was a commentator, hosted OSU and UO commencement exercises, emceed live organ concerts from the Whiteside Theatre, lobbied Oregon's politicians for funding, traveled to help other states with their early efforts in educational broadcasting and, I'm proud to say, hired women. Yes, they mostly hosted what was called women's programming; to quote from my father's book, *The Remembered Years,* that meant radio programs focused on "homemaking, household administration, household finance, household art, household science, and physical education for women." But at least women were on the air, and not all women's programming centered on the home.

I miss the past – their past. I know it well because my father shot a lot of 8mm home movies beginning in the 1930s and I have my mother's five-year diary from the early 1940s. They documented their travels, including the months they spent in New York City in the summer of 1941 while my father was at a radio playwriting workshop at NYU where he worked and studied with radio great Norman Corwin and novelist Charles R. Jackson, author of *The Lost Weekend*. Bearing a resemblance to Clara Bow, my mother could style her hair and sew dresses, copying styles of the day. She looked glamorous hanging on to her hat in the breeze at the top of the Empire State Building.

My father looked like orchestra leader Paul Whiteman – rotund, some years with a moustache, some years not. No teenage girl wants to be constantly told she looks like her short, heavy father, but I was. One person called me a dead ringer. To tell the truth, I was never *that* embarrassed.

My parents were always busy. To read my mother's diaries is to read about my dad's work at KOAC, his teaching, and my mother helping grade papers. She writes about their work on the house, adding a greenhouse, reading aloud to each other, visiting my father's family in Eugene, my mother's in Corvallis and Tidewater, church responsibilities, my mother's many decades as a Red Cross Gray Lady, her taking care of a friend with postpartum depression (and taking care of her baby too), bicycling to town, cooking, canning, visiting neighbors, sewing, writing letters to family, going to the occasional movie or play, helping out during a live orchestral production or play at KOAC, and nearly every day seeing close friends for a meal or dessert, or just to visit. That was their life before children, and it didn't change that much when Sterling and I came along. As Sterling and I have concluded, we were loved but we weren't doted on.

My father wrote radio plays – two volumes were published – and had a stable of two hundred student actors who appeared in the live productions using sound effects equipment he had, naturally, built himself. I remember, when I was in fifth or sixth grade at Roosevelt School, opening a new literature textbook the first day of class and seeing on the table of contents page that a radio play written by my father was included. I think it was his play about Rip Van Winkle. They accomplished so much that when I think about it, it makes me regret all the distractions we have now.

Sterling and I sometimes appeared on *Choo-Choo Charlie*, a children's program that KOAC-TV began in 1957. Choo-Choo Charlie was really speech and language expert Charlie Callaci dressed as a train engineer. In one photo, two or three rows of children, including Sterling and me, are sitting on risers. Everyone is listening attentively, except me. I'm trying to get the attention of the boy in front of me.

My parents had first rented a little house near Roosevelt School with a fish pond in the backyard. They decided they wanted to build a house. My dad went down to the bank and told the president, "Lucille and I want to build" and described the lot, a beautiful spot just a couple of blocks west. The back of the house, with the gate and trellis, would be on Western Avenue. The front of the house, with bay windows in the living room and dining room, and an octagon window in the master bath, would face Philomath Road. The president of the bank said, "Well, Jimmie, you get some two by fours up, and come back in and I'll give you a loan."

My dad, who could build anything, plumb anything, wire anything – although sometimes the likeliest light switch didn't operate what common sense said it should – got the foundation in and went back to the bank, got the loan, and finished the house. My mother helped with the building and painting, but her creativity was inside, as who we would call the hostess, with skills that I think died with her: perfect taste in décor, place settings, guest lists, menus, and creating an atmosphere. During the Depression and WWII, she knew how to do a lot with very little.

I loved their stories, especially the one about how after my dad completed the greenhouse, an elephant from the circus encamped across Philomath Road escaped and found the hose and faucet in the greenhouse. The noise roused my father out of bed. I can hear him saying, "Lucille, there's an elephant in the yard!" and the fun they must have had telling the story for years to come.

Sterling and I had freedom children don't have today. We could leave for hours, explore the OSU campus just a couple of blocks away, and crawl under the fence into the stadium, visit the Horner Museum in the basement of Gill Coliseum, and hang around the KOAC studios. One summer day, Sterling walked downtown barefoot, so of course I did too. The pavement was blistering hot but he didn't seem to notice so I pretended I didn't either.

I was a tomboy, and my parents permitted me to be. My father spent endless hours playing catch with me, and checkers, and driving our ski boat while I progressed from two skis to one. On Saturdays I would go with him to Jim the Fix'R, the bicycle-handyman shop on 2nd Street, borrowed by Bernard Malamud for his book, *The Fixer*.

We were not without problems. I tried to hear what my mother and brother were talking about in his room for hours at a time. I had a secret. My father built me a playhouse in the side yard, big enough for me and a friend or two. The exterior was painted whatever our home was at the time – usually yellow or pink – with window boxes. By the time I was ten, it was primarily where I could go to eat. I don't know if my mother knew I was sneaking food, but she knew I was big for my age. One summer she sat with me as I ate the same lunch every day: saltines and canned sardines. I still can't face a sardine.

A neighbor told my mother one of her daughters had eaten an entire pie; they must have been talking about daughters and their eating habits. I don't know why my mother passed on the story to me, but I'm sorry to say it put an idea in my head. I wouldn't have to sneak food item by item – I could sneak large amounts. And I did. I usually bought the food I needed at Kaiser's Market a couple of blocks away. It made me less lonely and filled me with something intangible I needed. I think my mother was worried about me. I don't think she was ashamed of me. But when I look at photographs now of my childhood, I see that I was not obese. I was never skinny, but I looked solid and I loved sports. I think my mother feared I would have my dad's weight problems. I look a lot like the women on his side of the family: strong, capable, and anything but slender. You'll have to take my word for it that this is not what sent me to therapy and that I believe she did the best she could.

My mother described her life as "charmed." I cannot call mine that, but I have been fortunate. When I was in my late teens and in my twenties, and beginning to make contacts and plan for a career in broadcasting, my father would send me out the door saying, "Tell them who you are." Sometimes I did – I would tell someone I was Jimmie Morris' daughter – and sometimes I didn't. The most important name I could drop was my dad's. But I wanted to depend on myself to get wherever I was going. I knew he was saying *Be who you are*. I knew he was saying they were handing me the independence to be anything I wanted to be.

At my father's memorial service in 1995, I talked about his influence. He played baseball as a boy, so I liked baseball. He played the alto sax, so I took it up. He worked in broadcasting, and that is what I wanted to do. He wrote plays and I have. He wrote books and I do. I didn't do these things to win his approval; I did them because he had so much fun. But it is my mother's presence I feel every day. I am more like her than I ever knew. She was the spunk in their relationship. Her head was always in a newspaper or book. I inherited my sense of curiosity from her, the talent for questioning anything and everything. My mother and I truly got to know each other after my father died.

I used to think Corvallis hadn't prepared me for the wider world. Now I think it did. When I spent years grieving over the deaths of two young husbands, over not having children, over life not being what I assumed it would be, and over the highs and many lows of a career in journalism, the confidence that got me through it was what I learned in my hometown. My parents are largely responsible for that. But I think the town is too. It gave me a home that was beyond an address — 1850 Western Avenue.

THE CAMPAIGN

In 1968, Oregon's presidential primary and other primaries in the West were more important than they are today. Many states had primaries scattered during the spring months. Now, states get on the bandwagon to stage early, influential, attention-grabbing primaries or caucuses.

My classmates couldn't vote, but it would be the last presidential election when teenagers couldn't. On March 10, 1971, the Twenty-Sixth Amendment to the Constitution was passed, lowering the voting age to eighteen.

After President Lyndon Johnson announced on March 31, 1968, that he would not run for re-election, the Democratic primary race changed quickly. Eugene McCarthy had announced his campaign in November 1967, and was getting solid support from college students. Robert F. Kennedy announced on March 16 he was running. When Johnson bowed out, Vice President Hubert Humphrey announced on April 27 and picked up labor support Johnson would have won.

It was exciting when some of the candidates announced they would campaign in Corvallis. Richard Nixon was the first. Some 7,000 people went to Gill Coliseum to hear him on April 24, 1968, give "a major political address," according to the *G-T*. A long story on Nixon – by Mike Bradley – called the candidate "genial and relaxed." Bradley described the setting as "a carnival atmosphere of colored balloons," with waving campaign signs, a peppy six-piece band made up of Portland high school students, and the "harsh lights of television cameras." The candidate outlined his views on the nation's foreign and domestic problems and then took questions. Our class invited Nixon to a potluck dinner the night he was in Corvallis. He sent a telegram with his apologies. He would be busy speaking at a spaghetti dinner at Salem's McNary High School.

The candidate was photographed shaking hands with "a button-wearing admirer, obviously too young to vote." The boy was Steve Jacobs, younger brother of my classmate Dave Jacobs. Dan Dickason went to hear Nixon; so did Donella, who got a story and a *High-O-Scope* editorial out of it.

While waiting in the lobby of Gill Coliseum to catch a look at Richard Nixon, I and the two high school girls standing with me were approached by a Nixon aide who asked us to move over a few feet so that we could be background for pictures taken of Nixon. Feeling pleasantly surprised as the aide moved us over, we were somewhat shocked when the aide said, and I quote, "we got to block the old people out." Eugene McCarthy and Robert Kennedy appeal to the younger generation, but Nixon has to recruit supporters in the younger people.

The real excitement was when Robert Kennedy came to Corvallis on May 27. We were in the middle of preparations for graduation. Judy Appelman, Donella, and Dan were among the students who heard RFK speak. Kennedy was on a train trip campaigning through Oregon. He was photographed walking on an Oregon beach and like Nixon, Kennedy spoke at OSU. He also made an appearance on the steps of the Benton County Courthouse. "He was mostly railing against Nixon," Dan remembers. A photograph in the *G-T* showed Kennedy being presented with a jar of honey by OSU student Karen Peterson, who was wearing a tiara. She had recently been named Queen Bee by the state's beekeepers.

Donella campaigned door to door for McCarthy, who did not come to Corvallis, and also for Wayne Morse, Oregon's

Democratic US Senator and one of only two senators to vote against US involvement in Vietnam.

On May 17, the *High-O-Scope* reported on how students in CHS Modern Problems classes would vote if they could. Of students who voted Democratic, 45 percent voted for Robert Kennedy, 41 percent for McCarthy, and 11 percent for Hubert Humphrey. Of students who voted Republican, 45 percent voted for Nelson Rockefeller, 39 percent for Richard Nixon, and 13 percent for Ronald Reagan. Three percent voted for George Wallace, who was running as a member of the American Independent Party. There were a number of write-in candidates, including comedian Pat Paulsen (two votes); President Lyndon Johnson, who had declared he was not running for re-election (three votes); and Fred Halstead, of the Socialist Workers Party (three votes).

Oregon's presidential primary was held May 28, 1968. Eugene McCarthy won 44 percent of the state's Democratic votes to Robert Kennedy's 38 percent. Richard Nixon won 65.1 percent of Oregon's Republican primary votes to Ronald Reagan's 20.4 percent. I think that's the year my parents voted for Nelson Rockefeller, who collected 11.6 percent of the state's Republican primary votes.

Eight days after he was in Corvallis, Robert Kennedy, on the night of our high school graduation, won California's Democratic presidential primary.

GRADUATION

It might be an urban myth – or, in our case, a small-town myth – that the idea of the all-night party was born after two CHS students died in a car accident after graduation or a prom. Alcohol was involved, of course. It is hard to pin down the truth because other towns across America think it originated with them. A Corvallis student was killed in a car accident around graduation time in the early 1960s, but the all-night CHS party by then had existed for years. It kept us busy, and out of cars. During the class of 1968 all-night party, following our graduation at Gill Coliseum, we were bused to various activities around town.

Five hundred-twenty-five of us would graduate, according to the *High-O-Scope,* which had reported on little else leading up to the end of the school year. There was the junior-senior prom, awards ceremonies, special meetings for seniors, baccalaureate, parties, picnics, and commencement rehearsals. At one of the awards assemblies, I was surprised by two honors I didn't know existed: the *High-O-Scope*'s Most Valuable Staff Member and Outstanding Service. I've always assumed I had my parents' Ford Galaxy to thank, the car I damaged parking at Seaton's, because I could be depended on to take people and newspaper copy back and forth to the *G-T*.

Alice Henderson was honored as the girl who Contributed Most to Corvallis High, and Tom Norton was named Most Congenial and Boy of the Year. Both were named Outstanding Seniors and won Kiwanis service scholarships to put toward college.

Mark was named a national merit scholarship finalist and ranked in the top five percent of our state's high school seniors. He had been accepted early to Stanford, and blew off much of spring term, especially after he was cut from the basketball team because of the length of his hair. He spent some of the time he wasn't in class driving to the coast with friends where they would drink. A girl he knew forged notes from his parents for him. One time when he really was sick, she had to write a real excuse note, in case the handwriting was compared.

In addition to the awards ceremonies, there was the senior picnic at Avery Park, followed by baccalaureate at Gill Coliseum, and finally commencement. We probably took our turn cleaning up Dixon Creek because it was a senior tradition. We had bequests to write. One of the final issues of the *High-O-Scope* devoted pages to dozens of bequeaths such as:

I, Stan Selfridge, will to Mr. Pinion my typing ability and my ability to botch up the income and expense books. I also will to Pam Paul all of my pencils and to her and Patty Wilson my bookkeeping knowledge of which the former has little of her own. To Mr. Saari my "senioritis" and the use of my middle name.

We, Tom Norton and Alice Henderson, will Kathy Dodson and John Overholser (next year's Spartan Spirit writers) five minutes each Wednesday before twelve o-clock to write the column and get it down.

I, Donella Russell, being a loud sound, do hearby will a 2x10 Coachman ad without the picture in it to Jeff Valentine, my real eyelashes to Wendy Gaehler, my car troubles and dictatorial personality to the next High-O-Scope editor, LaJuana Bell.

We, Morris (Bruce), Goheen and Koelling will our suave, refined and casual personalities and our knack for combining business and pleasure to Dave Oldfield and any other group of people who can handle them.

We, Becky Morris and Margret Murphy, hereby leave our knowledge, talent, and philosophy of scuba diving to our child successor, Kelly Lou Tharp. May she swim evermore in our bubbles.

One of Donella's last editorials was a thank you to the CHS administration for the absence of a dress code, for making our school probably the most liberal and responsible in the state, and for "letting us be ourselves and helping us to become the responsible adults of tomorrow."

There was also a lengthy article summarizing the three years our class had been at the high school, starting in 1965-66 as sophomores. The story mentioned class officers, members of the rally squad, the casts of dramatic productions, homecoming queens, exchange students, class skits, new courses, and how our athletic teams did during the three years. There was no mention of deaths, either of Dick Kitchel or of Steve Jeppsen, who had died when we were juniors.

Alice was the yearbook editor and she wanted to include a full page memoriam to Dick, like the 1967 yearbook gave to Steve, who died in a motorcycle accident. On the page before our junior class photos there was a large photo of Steve with some words from St. Francis of Assisi. But the faculty advisor discouraged Alice from calling attention to Dick's death or giving him a full-page dedication like Steve had. She proceeded as best she could. On the page after our senior portraits, Alice included a photo of Dick taken as he worked under the hood of a car in a class and also his senior class photo.

She also included the famous words of John Donne, written in 1624 as part of *Devotions Upon Emergent Occasions.* We know it better as the work that begins "No man is an island" and concludes "never send to know for whom the bell tolls; it tolls for thee." The line that has always stayed with me is "any man's death diminishes me." As opposed to Steve's yearbook page, Dick had to share a page with other photos and a long list of names of students who didn't have a senior picture. Some wondered if the school administration was embarrassed that Dick had been murdered.

The *Gazette-Times* covered our commencement – after all, we were the only high school in town. The school choir sang "The Impossible Dream" and the speaker was Thomas Thetford, son of my favorite teacher Robert Thetford, who encouraged me in his journalism and speech courses. Tom, Student Body President in 1965-66, was "fresh from Harvard" where he was pre-law. He told us we were second-class citizens because we couldn't vote, but we should be out campaigning for candidates we believed in. And he laid our frustrations, which he said were demonstrated in riots and use of marijuana and other drugs, at the feet of the World War II generation who were running things. A letter to the *G-T* a day or two later took issue with Tom's speech, saying we should not blame our parents for our problems.

Dick's good friend Dawn Seavy was back in town from Texas to watch our class graduate. In the two years since she left, she had been married, divorced, earned her GED, and was the mother of a ten month old. She had broken her leg two weeks earlier and was in a cast and on crutches. She was feeling melancholy about seeing the kids she had grown up with. "I remember sitting in the balcony looking down on all these people I'd gone to school with since kindergarten, knowing most of them but not really belonging. It was a strange feeling."

Few of us probably thought of Dick that night. The murder investigation stalled after the police could no longer put pressure on Doug Hamblin. Would it become what Mike Bradley implied in his *G-T* article of several months before, one of those cases that went unsolved and unpunished?

Our all-night party, titled "Passport to the Future," was held at the Elks Lodge where we boarded a pretend cruise ship, the SS Finale. There was an 11 p.m. buffet, a 4:15

a.m. breakfast, pool tables, and dancing to music played by The Patriots and The Ingredients Unknown. We could play miniature golf, bowl, or swim. The Whiteside Theatre replaced the film *In Cold Blood* for one night to show a Bob Hope-Phyllis Diller comedy. Margret and I were photographed by the *G-T* as "enjoying the Latin America atmosphere in the Mexican Art Gallery" where a Bingo game was also going on. Margret appears to be holding fast to a very large bottle of gin, but that is impossible. Honest. Some graduates had alcohol, even with parental chaperones scattered at the party sites. Alice spent the night, she said, "with alcohol between my legs." A friend had smuggled in some liquor in a small vial and shared it around.

Alice and Tom broke up at the all-night party. It wasn't a teary, dramatic breakup. It was an acknowledgement that they were going their separate ways, at least for a while. Their last big evening had been the junior-senior prom. Now, Alice would go to the University of Oregon in Eugene; Tom was joining the army. He still hadn't told her that he was gay. "I didn't want to lose her as a friend," he said.

Just a few weeks earlier, he had driven alone to Fort Lewis, the army base near Tacoma, Washington. Tom wanted to be a pilot and he thought joining the military would make him straight. At Fort Lewis, he passed tests, took a flight physical, and signed a contract guaranteeing him a slot in flight school in Dallas, Texas. The day he joined up was the first good night's sleep he'd had in as long as he could remember. "I was so happy," he said. "I was going to be normal. I'd be a man if I joined the army. I thought I could fly away from what I was feeling. I was so naïve. I didn't know I couldn't change." His mother may have suspected Tom's secret. As he was about to enter the military, she said that if they asked him if he had any homosexual tendencies, he should answer no.

After the break up with Tom at the party, Alice found comfort talking to a fellow classmate. He was Lutheran and talked to her about God and she listened. He shared meanings from scriptures she'd never really thought about before. When she arrived at the University of Oregon in the fall, she would visit a number of campus ministries looking for a faith that spoke to her.

Most of us would spend the summer earning some money and preparing to go to college, because that was what was expected of us. Dan worked at the farm crops department at OSU, then left to attend Portland State University. Donella canned beets at Blue Lake Packers and worked at OSU banquets and at the campus soda fountain. She moved to Portland to attend PSU. Mark spent the summer as he had spent his spring, wasting time before he attended Stanford, where he continued his father's legacy of social justice, participating in sit-ins, marches, and acts of civil disobedience on campus. I may have worked in an office on campus that summer; once upon a time, my family spent nearly three months of the year at our cabin at Odell Lake, but my visits there began to be curtailed with college and marriage and career. Sterling was finishing at OSU and going into the navy – a deal my father had made with the army recruiter who had wanted to draft my brother. That fall I stayed in town and started at OSU. I had a disastrous freshman year, dropped out, and returned later. Alice spent the summer working as a roller skating carhop at The Big O. Tom was off to basic training at Fort Polk, Louisiana, then to army helicopter flight training. Two 1968 CHS graduates would die in Vietnam — Scott Cochran and Vernon Schrock.

On the last night our class was together, as we ate, sipped forbidden alcohol, played pool, and danced, Robert Kennedy was winning the California presidential primary. Just after midnight, after addressing his supporters in Los Angeles, he cut through a hotel kitchen and was shot three times. Word circulated through our graduation gathering. Kennedy had been in Corvallis the week before. Some of us had seen him. It was not our first assassination, but he was as close to a hero as we had. He died the next day. That summer, as we began to go out into the world and away from Corvallis, America erupted in race riots, and anti-war and women's liberation demonstrations. In August, the Democratic National Convention in Chicago was the scene of violence, political turbulence, and civil unrest.

Alice had chosen as the theme for the yearbook "Perspectives ... To Each His Own." Music had been an influence in our lives as teenagers in the 1960s. Simon and Garfunkel's "I Am a Rock" had made an impression on her. "I felt that the white and black answers of the 1950s were blurring in the 1960s," she said. "There was no one right answer or perspective. The world was becoming smaller and we were beginning to accept different ideas, thoughts and opinions.

"It felt like the world was coming apart," she said.

NOW

....

COLD CASE

In 2008, Detective Tyson Poole of the Corvallis Police Department inherited a cold case. It was the 1967 murder of Dick Kitchel. He was assigned to help another detective take a look at the murder, the first look in forty years. Poole is methodical and organized and didn't like the less than ideal methods of the other detective. He didn't want to step on toes so he waited a few months until the other detective left the department, then plunged in.

Poole was thirty-six years old. He had grown up in Bly, Oregon, a tiny town in southern Oregon famous for being the only place on the US mainland hit by enemy attack causing fatalities during World War II. It happened in May 1945, when a Japanese balloon bomb, which had landed in some woods, was found by picnickers and exploded. Poole served in the army in Italy as an airborne paratrooper. After the service, he attended college in Bend, Oregon, and began his police career as a reserve deputy with the Deschutes County Sheriff's Office. He was hired by the Corvallis Police Department in 2001 as a patrol officer and worked his way up to detective.

The way Poole organizes a cold case is to:
1. Locate evidence
2. Talk to everyone involved in the case
3. Talk to people who were present at the time of the murder

It seems simple, logical. But Poole's experience is that being methodical pays off in solving and closing cases. There were problems with this one from the beginning. Police departments are required to keep evidence in a homicide forever. What remained of the case was poorly organized. A lot was missing.

The department was overworked dealing with contemporary cases. In 2008, detectives had just closed the Brooke Wilberger case. The nineteen year old had finished her freshman year at Brigham Young in Salt Lake City when she was abducted from her sister's apartment in Corvallis on May 24, 2004. It took four years for the department to find the man who had killed her and left her body in the woods, and have him extradited to Corvallis. The department had also closed a cold case, the murder of Greg Kirkelie, arresting his widow for his murder twenty-three years before.

Poole thought the passage of time discouraged others from wanting to work on the Kitchel case. "I didn't like that it was left to sit for so long, and this was a very solvable case, in my opinion. I couldn't help but wonder how many other detectives this passed through who didn't even look at it.

"The first thing I wanted to know was: was there any evidence?" Poole told me. "I spent time going through case files, I canvassed the police department and the police archives. I went to the DA's office." The original police report was aging and had never been photocopied. In fact, it had never been officially filed, scanned, or logged into the department's computerized management system over the years. What there was had been passed around in an old binder. He made a working copy in order to preserve the original pages.

Poole found the 1960s audio recording equipment, but the reels of tape with interviews of Doug Hamblin and others were not just missing — they had never even been transcribed. Photos from the crime scene, taken when Dick's body was pulled from the river, had never been developed and the film was missing. Dick's clothing was gone. Today, police departments have areas where they dry out evidence and preserve it, but in 1967, preservation meant storing items in paper bags. Dick's clothes, the tape recordings, and the film may have all gone into paper bags that were tossed out over the years. "Where did the evidence go?" Poole wanted to know. "There was a breach."

And yet Poole knew a lot of resources had been put into the investigation. The police had returned to Doug time after time, requesting multiple polygraph exams. He found those reports. He praised Detectives Montgomery and Hockema for their "extremely detailed notes." "They wanted to solve it," he said. Still, Poole reached a conclusion. "I could not understand why they didn't arrest him."

Poole, trained in forensics and DNA gathering, modern police methods that didn't exist in 1967, was alarmed that Doug's car was never given a thorough going-over. "They looked at Doug's car, but did not seize it. Today, the car would immediately be seized. I would have talked to the other passengers – who was in the car and what was going on? Were Dick and Doug arguing? What were they talking about?" Although a body found in water is not like a death on dry land, Poole wished there had been the technology then to have done more. "The first thing I would have done is swabbed Dick's neck to see if Hamblin's DNA was on it," and he would have examined Dick's clothing carefully. Even forty years later, "I wanted the stuff he was wearing," Poole said. It might have contained Doug's DNA. Maybe it would have been evidence that could result in an arrest.

He was stymied trying to find people. He wanted to find Pat Hockett, the Everts' babysitter who knew everybody in the complicated case. But there was only the old California address from when Jim Montgomery interviewed her in February 1968. He found other loose ends in the case file that had never been followed up on.

Poole devised a game plan. First and foremost, he would revisit Doug's original statements, then question him and lock him into his story. He checked with current Chief Deputy DA Christian Stringer to ask if they could question

Doug without an attorney present, and if they could compel his minister to talk. The answer to both was *yes*. All the while, he was digging, he believed that Doug probably knew the case was being looked at. "He had to have known it was coming. You'd have to go your entire life wondering if it would be re-opened."

On March 25, 2008, Poole sat down with the retired detectives, Jim Montgomery and Bill Hockema, and former DA Frank Knight. Three other Corvallis Police Department detectives joined the group.

They talked about why Ralph Kitchel hadn't reported his son missing until several days had passed, about how the reel to reel tape recordings and clothes were probably lost when offices moved. They discussed why the case was never presented to the grand jury, the polygraph results, talking to Doug's minister, and looking at Doug's hands and body for injuries ten days after the fight would have taken place. There was Doug's car with the broken passenger door, his admission to the detectives that he had reached into the car and wrapped an arm around Dick's neck to pull him out of the vehicle, and his demonstration for police. They discussed how Doug lied about the coat, first saying he didn't know anything about it. Poole thought that if Doug was innocent, he would have come forward immediately with the coat, not waited for the police to ask about it. As for the chain Montgomery thought he saw around Dick's neck when the body was pulled ashore, no one else remembered it and it was not mentioned in the autopsy report.

Montgomery, Hockema, and Knight believed Doug might have killed Dick accidentally, as he tried to pull Dick out of his car. Poole didn't think so. He had read the autopsy report many times. "Dick had black eyes, he had been beaten to that extent. No, Hamblin did not accidentally kill him. But he may not have *intended* to kill him. He went too far. He probably was angry at the moment, found Dick was dead, and thought, 'Oh crap.'" Poole thought Doug had driven Dick somewhere, maybe not 4th and B Street. The fight started when he tried to get Dick to leave the car. Maybe the fight started in the front seat; that's where he blackened Dick's eyes. Then pulling him out of the car caused the strangulation.

Poole left the meeting with a feeling that Montgomery and Hockema agreed that Knight could have presented the case to a grand jury. Poole didn't think it was too late, and was going to try to make it happen. He turned his focus to what was new, what he had learned from his meeting with Montgomery, Hockema, and Knight. The fact that Doug Hamblin had confided in his minister was not in the original police report. Poole had learned more about how Doug demonstrated pulling Dick out of his car. Poole vowed to talk to people who had never been questioned, to talk with Hamblin, and to follow-up on notes buried in the original file.

A few days later, on April 4, 2008, Poole met with John Lee, a man who had contacted the police department in the 1970s saying he had information about Dick's murder. A note with his name was stuck in the back of the original case file. Poole met him at the Corvallis Police Department. Lee told Poole that for years he had lived across the street in Albany from Doug Hamblin's first wife, Teresa. He said that Teresa had told him many times that Doug had confessed to her that he had killed Dick. Teresa and Doug had divorced in 1966, before Dick's murder, but had a daughter and re-married briefly, so there were many opportunities for them to talk over the years. Lee had urged Teresa to talk to the police but she refused, telling him that she was afraid of Doug. Lee knew Doug and Poole asked what he was like. Lee repeatedly described him as "wild," drinking a lot, driving fast, doing "crazy stuff." Lee said it would not surprise him if he had killed Dick.

Poole found an address for Teresa in Albany. He would see her, then go to the district attorney's office to make a case for charging Doug Hamblin with murder. But he learned that Teresa had died in 1990. Three years passed.

Tyson Poole was pulled away and assigned to other cases. He also studied to be a computer forensics examiner. He returned to the Kitchel case in 2011. On May 5, 2011, he and another detective, Bryan Rehnberg, met with Martha Taylor at her house in Albany. Martha told them the story of her going to see an attorney in a child custody case and how he called Doug "the only person in Corvallis to get away with murder." Doug had told Martha that he was last person to see Dick but always denied having anything to do with his death. She said during their marriage she came to believe he was a pathological liar. She said she thought he was full of rage and capable of murder. Doug didn't like it when she brought up the subject of the murder. "He never fully admitted to killing Kitchell [sic], but she has believed all this time that he was responsible," Poole wrote in his notes.

And then Martha Taylor told the detective something he didn't know: Doug Hamblin was dead. He had collapsed and died of a heart attack at his home in Corvallis on November 28, 2008. He was 64. Poole was stunned. "I remember being very disappointed when I verified he had passed because I was hoping to bring the survivors of this closure. It felt like I let them down because I was too late. I was very much looking forward to speaking with Doug for myself."

Poole continued his investigation. He thought he had probable cause for the DA to take it to a grand jury. It wasn't unheard of when a suspect was deceased. It would mean a panel of Doug's peers who reviewed the case believed there was enough evidence to conclude he committed the murder. But it was too late. "The DA said they couldn't afford to, it was too expensive and time consuming."

As for the investigation, it is what is called "closed exceptionally," meaning it is closed because the district attorney declined to prosecute or because of the death of the offender; in this case, the presumed offender. Closed exceptionally means no further investigative means will be spent on the case.

Poole left the Corvallis Police Department in 2013 and is now a police officer in Bend, Oregon. He continues to think about the Kitchel case. "There was no doubt in my mind that Doug Hamblin killed Dick Kitchel," Poole told me. "There was more work to be done. It takes the DA's office to push. I don't think they purposely dropped it. But I think there was a lack of interest. They let it be forgotten."

THE DETECTIVES
AND THE DA #2

On November 2, 2015, I sat down with Jim Montgomery, Bill Hockema, and Frank Knight at Hockema's home in the hills west of Corvallis. I had talked with each of them on the phone and Knight once in person, but I wanted to get them together to see if they would prompt each other with memories about the Dick Kitchel murder investigation. Over coffee and cookies, they studied copies I had of the police report and packets I had made for each of them with stories from the *Gazette-Times* about the murder.

Now in their late seventies and early eighties, the three were immediately comfortable, as if they had seen each other the day before. In fact, they do run into each other in town. Hockema and Montgomery live in the same wooded area. The three have known each other more than fifty years. They remembered the case clearly, nearly minute by minute, day by day. They also remember it is the only murder they never closed. The bulk of the investigation lasted about six months. After that, leads dried up and the detectives were assigned to other cases. But they knew who had killed Dick.

"There were two reasons why we were convinced Doug Hamblin was responsible," Jim Montgomery said. "One was Hamblin's minister, who said if we were looking at Doug, 'we were headed in the right direction.' The other was the third polygraph, when the state police polygraph expert found that Hamblin was 'probably responsible' for the murder."

There was also the accepted theory that the last person to see the murdered person alive was responsible for their death. They could find no one – not Dick's father or a friend or a stranger – who had seen Dick after he got into Doug's car. As for Detective Poole believing Doug could have been arrested in 1967-68? "They wanted to say they had solved a cold case," Hockema said, sounding skeptical.

Doug must have known the first two polygraphs were inconclusive. After the third one, they told him it had "come up dirty." That's when his attorney warned them to either bring charges or back off. It would have taken a confession to charge him. "He would have had to say that he did it," Montgomery said. "We hoped his conscience would lead to confession." It never did.

The three are convinced that Dick's death may have been an accident, that Doug didn't *know* when Dick got into his car that night that he was going to murder him. After he dropped the other two boys off, he and Dick struggled. Dick had moved to the right front passenger seat of the DeSoto, the one by the broken door. Dick was drunk and Doug had been drinking. Dick was being stubborn, who knows why. The two struggled and Dick was strangled as Doug removed him from the car. If it was an accident that occurred during a fight, Doug would have faced manslaughter charges. But there just wasn't enough evidence, according to Knight, who was worrying about the potential of double jeopardy. Tyson Poole continues to believe that Dick was so badly beaten it had to have been more than an accident.

Doug remained on their radar over the years. "This guy became one of our early druggies, mostly marijuana," Knight said. "We're not talking high society here," Hockema added.

They remembered how disturbing they found Ralph Kitchel, who was hostile to them, never once contacting the department to ask how the investigation was going. "He did not seem sad," Hockema said. "He did not like the police. 'I know my rights!' he'd tell us."

Montgomery remembered clearly being at the Willamette River when Dick's body was pulled from the water. The body was black, ugly, and bloated. He still remembers seeing a chain around Dick's neck that had become caught in his mouth as the body became bloated. It might have been a good luck charm or a St. Christopher's medal. Montgomery is surprised there is no mention of it in the police report or autopsy report. I asked the girls Dick dated if they remembered him wearing a chain and they didn't. Finally, Montgomery decided the chain might have been a memory from a different case.

One of the clearest memories all three have is of going to the Everts' house the evening of the day Dick's body was found. They found almost the same cast of characters as had been present ten days before at the party – Juddi and Paul Everts, Doug Hamblin, and Mel Plemmons. The four were playing a drinking game. They showed no reaction when the detectives told them Dick had been found murdered.

As for the lost evidence, Knight thinks his office didn't have the money to transcribe the reel to reel tapes of their interviews with Doug. They were probably lost when his office moved. Still, he doesn't remember a big revelation from Doug during a taping. If there was one, they would have charged him. Today, the men believe that a relative of Doug's, whom they never spoke with, probably knows more than anyone about what happened.

I asked them about what I heard some classmates suggest, that the murder would have been solved if Dick's parents were prominent. "We like to solve cases," Montgomery insisted. "We were frustrated. We would go home at night asking ourselves, 'what can we do?'"

Leads dried up and eventually they got other assignments. Frank Knight kept telling them there was not enough to make an arrest. He stands by that decision.

EPILOGUE

Seaton's is gone. So is Roosevelt School, A&W, The Big O, Wagner's, McGregor's 5&10, Riverview Marina, The Gables, Lipman's, Tony's House of Music, Jim the Fix'r, CHS, and dozens of other places important to my childhood. The Whiteside Theatre is undergoing a slow restoration and is open one or two nights a week to show a movie. The Willamette River was cleaned up in 1972 and the salmon have returned. Walkers on a path along the riverfront pass restaurants, coffee roasters, microbreweries, bakeries, public art, and condos costing three-quarters of a million dollars. The Benton County Historical Society's Horner Museum, for decades tucked in a corner of the basement of Gill Coliseum, will have a new home by the river. Leading Floral moved and is 101 years old. The building it shared with Kitchel's Shoe Repair and Tots to Teens looks abandoned. Other buildings, the handsome ones at OSU, the First Christian Church, and the courthouse, are frozen in time, thank goodness. The Peacock Tavern, in its same home on 2nd Street since 1929, is now the Peacock Bar & Grill, known for its live music and breakfasts. The business district has sprawled to the north and south, but downtown Corvallis is still busy. Parts of Brigadoon endure, even with progress.

Five hundred-twenty-five of us graduated on June 4, 1968. There could be 525 answers to the question of how Dick's murder affected us. It must mean something that many of us have remembered him over the years. We remembered his death was unsolved and we assumed his father had killed him during a fight.

His death, and the nightmare year of 1968, made it more difficult for Corvallis to keep the larger world at arm's length. Some classmates went to Vietnam; some attended universities where student unrest was a part of life. There were higher profile crimes to come. Jerome Brudos, a Salem resident who came and went from Corvallis, was a serial killer and necrophiliac with a shoe fetish. Randall Woodfield, who killed young women up and down Interstate 5 from Washington to California, attacked two women in Corvallis, one of them Diana Eddins, who dated Dick Kitchel. One of Ted Bundy's earliest victims was Roberta Kathleen Parks, a student who disappeared from OSU May 6, 1974. One of several men suspected of being D.B. Cooper passed through town and attended a party in early November 1971.

For some of us, Dick's death confirmed our ideas about Corvallis and the importance of the status we were born to. It cemented ideas that Corvallis was a divided town, a town that sat out the 1960s.

I thought I had nothing in common with my classmates who told me they got out of town as soon as they could. I did too, and I only see it now. At age nineteen, I married the only boy I had ever dated. He went off to army boot camp and then Vietnam. I dropped out of college but eventually went back after an epiphany that I wanted to work in broadcasting, like my father. The boy and I divorced a year after he came back from Vietnam. No animosity, just too many years in young adulthood spent apart. I was happily married two more times – but widowed twice by age thirty-three. Friends, good ones, wondered out loud if I was jinxed or doomed. For me, much of life has been about what might have been.

The events of October 11-12, 1967, led to a murder that was an anomaly, even then. In the days before forensics, solving a crime depended on evidence: eyewitnesses, a weapon, fingerprints, a crime scene, a confession. The Kitchel case had none of those. There was no crime scene. Police only knew where Doug *said* he had pulled over his car to drop Dick off. There was no blood on a street or a sidewalk or by the river. There was nothing in the car. Police never knew where Dick had been killed. Ten days had passed since Dick disappeared and his body was found. If there was a crime scene, ten days had washed away any sign of it.

What do I think happened the night of October 11, 1967? I believe the theories of both Detective Tyson Poole, and Montgomery, Hockema, and Knight. I don't think Doug set out to kill Dick. There was a struggle, which grew into a bloody fight. Dick died, and Doug disposed of the body.

How, then, did Doug Hamblin live with himself? Badly. He drank, eventually stopped, but remained an angry man. He married and divorced several times. He was often in debt. If he ever did confess the murder to a wife, a brother, a minister, or a stranger, we will probably never know. He had a chance to become a better person, to atone for his mistakes. He never did.

Who and what would Dick have become? Maybe he would have stayed and raised a family in Corvallis. Maybe he would have moved away. I wish he had had the chance to find out who he could be. As one friend of his told me, "He was unfinished."

WHERE ARE THEY NOW

Jim Montgomery, Bill Hockema and Frank Knight
discussing the Kitchel murder case, November, 2015

Detective Sergeant Jim Montgomery and Captain Bill
Hockema retired on the same day, July 1, 1987, not for
sentimental reasons but because it was the end of a fiscal
year. Over the years, Montgomery worked with DA Frank
Knight on other important murder investigations, including
the stabbing death of OSU student Nancy Wyckoff, killed in
her dorm room on February 8, 1972.

Frank Knight was elected to the bench and served as
Benton County Circuit Court Judge from 1973–97. "I
preferred being DA to being on bench," he told me. "As DA,
I knew what was going on. As a judge, all you know is what
you hear in court."

NEWSMAN T. MICHAEL BRADLEY DIES

He was a member of the Corvallis Elks Lodge, the Kiwanis and Lions clubs, the Spring Hill Country Club and the Yawners Toastmaster club. He also belonged to Sigma Delta Chi and Cappa Tau Alpha.

The funeral service will be at 2 p.m. Tuesday in the chapel of McHenry Funeral Home, 206 N.W. 3th St. Burial will follow at the Oaklawn Memorial Park Cemetery.

Survivors include his wife, Mildred; two sons, Theron M. Bradley Jr., of Idaho Falls, Idaho and William A. Bradley, of Corvallis; a daughter, Alice L. Reinheimer, of Beaverton; a brother, Robert O. Bradley, of Albany; and three grandchildren, Theron M. Bradley III, of Idaho Falls, Idaho, Cody A. Reinheimer, of Beaverton and Cammillia A. Bradley, of Corvallis.

Remembrances may be made to Benton County Hospice in care of McHenry Funeral Home.

T Michael Bradley Fixture at the G T for 35 years

Mike Bradley retired in 1981 after 35 years at the *Gazette-Times* where he worked as a photographer, reporter, city and county beat reporter, chief political and investigative reporter, news editor, city editor, and eventually becoming

managing editor and editorial page editor. Bradley died in 1984 at age 68.

Alice Henderson Rampton graduated from the University of Oregon. Despite the wishes of her parents (who thought one Mormon daughter, Alice's sister, was enough), she joined the Church of Jesus

Alice Henderson

A MURDER IN MY HOMETOWN | 183

Christ of Latter-Day Saints. She co-founded a non-profit that benefits children in Ukraine who have disabilities or are poor. She is the co-author of *Finding Life After Losing One,* a book for parents who have lost a child, as she and her husband Mark did. They live in Corvallis.

Tom Norton

Tom Norton flew 1,861 medevac missions as a helicopter pilot in Vietnam, was shot down more times than he can remember, and awarded the Bronze Star for valor. He started medical school, but left to be a pilot in Alaska. When he was 27, he walked away from a crash that killed one passenger and injured another. Five hours later, he had a stroke. He remains partly paralyzed. Now a gay activist in Portland, he met Bao Nguyen, a Vietnamese refugee, in 1995. They married in 2004. Every year they go to Vietnam to do humanitarian work in orphanages. About his teenage years, he said, "It was a major disappointment for me to not have the nerve or guts to come out of the closet in high school."

Donella Russel

Donella Russell studied Arabic at Portland State University and worked for USAID, serving in Egypt, Russia, Pakistan, Ukraine, and Hungary. She lives in Portland.

Mark Goheen did both his undergraduate and graduate work at Stanford, has a PhD in Applied Math, and continues to work in the computer industry. He lives in Corvallis. His father, Harry Goheen, died on November 5, 1988. When the *Gazette-Times* remembered his activism and work for the NAACP and

Mark Goheen

ACLU, it related this story: As family and friends visited him during his last days they asked if there was anything they could do for him. He told them "Yes, go vote for Dukakis!" He died three days before the presidential election. He had already turned in his absentee ballot.

Ralph Kitchel and **Sylvia Kitchel** divorced and both remarried. Sylvia Kitchel died in 1996 and is buried next to Dick in Albany's Twin Oaks Memorial Gardens. A third plot bought by them when Dick died, presumably meant for Ralph, is unused. Ralph died in 2004 in Palm Springs, California. His obituary mentions three stepsons. There is no mention of the son who preceded him in death.

Judy Appelman

Joan Carey, Dick's mother, was married several times. She died in 1983.

Judy Appelman graduated from OSU and taught school in Portland. She lives in Bend. She says Dick's death has "haunted" her.

Paul Everts

Paul Everts and **Juddi Everts** settled in the Portland area. Juddi died in 2014, just days before they celebrated their 49th wedding anniversary. Paul is a real estate broker in Yamhill County, Oregon.

Judy Seavy Everts

Dawn Seavy Ashpole is a QuickBooks consultant in Portland. She still thinks about how Dick's life was cut short.

Dan Eckles bought Riverview Marina from his father in 1996 and moved it to

Donieta Seavy (Dawn Seavy Ashpole)

Albany. The business only survived a few more years. Dan works for a car dealership in Albany.

Bob Wadlow has been a teacher, school counselor, and school administrator. Dick's murder was "pretty traumatic" for him. His band The Patriots sometimes plays for class reunions.

Diana Eddins

Diana Eddins left home the day she turned 18. In 1981, she was working in a Corvallis fabric store when she was attacked. She picked Randall Woodfield, known as the I-5 Killer, out of a police lineup, helping to finally end his reign of murder.

Linda Niggebrugge Klinge was in the first class of women to attend the police academy in Oregon and joined the Linn County Sheriff' Office in 1970. She worked for 20 years for United Steelworkers of America and was the president of Oregon's NOW chapter. She lives in Corvallis.

Dean Beaudreau attended OSU and worked as an accountant. He has lived in Hawaii, Europe, Portland, and Sunriver, Oregon. Dean is optimistic about the man Dick might have become. "I think he would have done well. He struggled in school, but he would have had a good life."

Jeff Almgren is the Clinical Pharmacist for bone marrow and stem cell transplants at the VA Medical Center in Seattle, and Clinical Professor at the University of Washington School of Pharmacy.

Doug Hamblin died of a heart attack in Corvallis in 2008. He was 64. His ashes were scattered at the Oregon coast and at a lake in the Cascades.

Martha Taylor divorced Doug Hamblin in 1995 after fifteen years of marriage. He married again a month later and she never saw him again. She later remarried and worked at Hewlett-Packard. She lives in Corvallis. Although Doug never confessed the murder to her, she thinks it haunted him.

Rebecca Morris

Rebecca Morris is the *New York Times* bestselling author of *A Killing in Amish Country, If I Can't Have You, Ted and Ann,* and other books. She attended OSU, graduated with a degree in Journalism from Seattle University, and has an MFA in Creative Writing from Brown University. She worked in broadcast and print journalism in New York City, Seattle, Washington, and Portland, Oregon. She lives in Seattle.

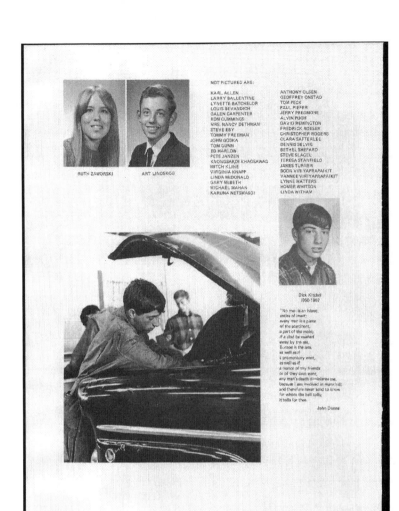

RUTH ZAWORSKI   ART LINDSKOG

Dick Kitchel
1950-1967

"No man is an island,
entire of itself;
every man is a piece
of the continent,
a part of the main;
if a clod be washed
away by the sea,
Europe is the less,
as well as if
a promontory were,
as well as if
a manor of thy friends
or of they own were;
any man's death diminishes me,
because I am involved in mankind;
and therefore never send to know
for whom the bell tolls;
it tolls for thee.

John Donne

92

Our yearbook tribute to Dick Kitchel

ACKNOWLEDGEMENTS

Thank you to the dozens of classmates who shared their memories of Dick Kitchel and of Corvallis with me. Happily, many I didn't know before have become good friends.

For my education into Corvallis' history I am enormously grateful to Mary Gallagher, Collections Manager, Benton County Museum, and to a Benton County Historical Society volunteer who wishes to be unnamed.

My thanks to the many people who spoke with me, most more than once, over the last three years:

Frank Knight, Jim Montgomery, Bill Hockema, James Tyson Poole, Roger Schmeltz, Alice Henderson Rampton, Mark Rampton, Tom Norton, Mark Goheen, Donella Russell, Bob Wadlow, Martha Taylor, Jeannine Frazier, Paul Everts, Dawn Seavy Ashpole, Judy Appelman, Diana Eddins Larrabee, Stan Selfridge, Linda Niggebrugge Klinge, Dan Eckles, Margo Eckles, Judy Eckles Jones, Dennis Jones, Jeff Almgren, Dean Beaudreau, Terry Garren, Margret Murphy, and Sterling Morris.

Thank you to others who helped with research or in other ways gave encouragement: Cathleen Lemke Wallace, Mary Gerard, Jim and Kristi Hammerquist, Joyce Kirk, Cheryl Wolfenberger, Linda MacIntyre Peter, Colleen Candee, Mike Terwilliger, Bob Ringo, Lois Hillemann, Connie Plants, Margaret Coon, Ginger Adams Otis, Kate Smith and Steph Cook.

Also thank you to Drew Lundgreen of McHenry Funeral Home, the Corvallis-Benton County Library, Salem Public Library, Oregon State University Special Collections and Archives Research Center, and the Corvallis Police Department.

I'm grateful to Steve Jackson and the editors, designers and entire staff at Wildblue Press for one of the best publishing experiences I've ever had.

And two important sources of information that never let me down:

Members of Corvallis High School Class of 1968 Facebook page

Members of "You Know You Are From Corvallis If…" Facebook page

The names Roger Bicks and John Lee are pseudonyms.

1.

An hour before sunset, Shaun Ware swung his white work truck right off Goodrick Drive into the Summit Industrial Park, a complex of metal buildings with tall garage doors. It was Sunday, Aug. 17, 2014, a warm summer evening in the high desert. Shadows enveloped the Tehachapi Pass, the mighty turbines in the windmill farm standing still in the light western breeze. Traffic roared by on Highway 58, cars and trucks shuttling between Bakersfield and the Mojave Desert. Every half hour, a long freight train from Burlington Northern Santa Fe Railway would rumble behind the complex.

Arriving for his overnight shift, Shaun pulled his truck up to a space with "BNSF" stenciled on the concrete parking block and immediately felt something was wrong. The metal door to the work area was closed. The day-shift responder, Robert Limon, would have kept it open to ventilate the stuffy garage during the 89-degree afternoon. Robert would have told him if he were out on a service call or making a food run.

Shaun raised the door with a remote opener. Robert's BNSF utility truck was parked next to his personal car, a silver Honda. Shaun walked into the garage along the right side of the truck. He nearly stepped on broken glass that appeared to have come from one of the fluorescent fixtures hanging from the 18-foot ceiling.

To his right, the door to the small office was wide open. That was wrong, too. The office door always stayed closed. The office appeared to have been ransacked. File drawers had been yanked open and papers strewn across the floor. A BNSF-issued Toshiba laptop was missing.

Shaun walked around the front of the work truck, which pointed toward the kitchenette against the back wall. The door of the small refrigerator was flung open. So was the door to the bathroom.

That's when he saw him.

Robert Limon was on the floor, his back slumped against the driver's side tire of the truck.

Shaun kneeled.

"Rob, what happened?" Shaun said. "Wake up, buddy."

Robert had a vacant look on his face, one eye closed, the other half opened. Blood had pooled beneath him. He didn't respond.

Panic gripped Shaun. He called 911 on his cell phone. He told the operator that he had found his coworker on the ground around a lot of blood and that he wasn't moving.

The operator asked if Shaun was willing to try CPR. He said yes. Following the operator's instructions, Shaun pulled Robert down flat on his back. He put his face close to Robert's. There was no breath. The operator asked Shaun to push his hands against Robert's chest to begin compressions.

One push and blood oozed out of Robert's mouth.

The operator told Shaun to get out of the building, now. He did, in a daze. The cell phone still to his ear with the 911 operator on the line, he wandered out to the asphalt parking area.

A man approached—somebody who worked in a neighboring unit—and asked Shaun what was going on.

"I think Rob's dead," Shaun told him.

Then it hit him. Shaun dropped to his knees and his body convulsed. He felt tears coming.

How long he was like this, he couldn't remember. The next thing he knew, he heard cars approaching. Sirens. Lights. He looked up and saw a woman in a sheriff's uniform.

Shaun pointed to the garage and said, "He has two kids."

2.

Two deputies from the Kern County Sheriff's Office fielded the 911 call at 6:46 p.m. for a "male found bleeding and not breathing" at 1582 Goodrick Drive, Tehachapi, Calif. They arrived in separate one-deputy patrol cars. Both had often seen the facility from the 58, but had never been on call there.

Goodrick Drive took them to a cul-de-sac with a driveway leading into the five buildings of the complex. Since it was a Sunday night, all of the garage doors were shut—save for one—and the place empty, except for the man crouched on the pavement.

Kern County Senior Deputy Marcus Moncur got there first. The 10-year veteran cop approached the man, who was shaking but saying nothing. A second, deputy, Anna Alvarez, a rookie patrol officer, arrived in her patrol car. Moncur asked her to stay with the man and talk to him while he checked out the garage 50 yards away.

There, the deputy saw the silver Honda and the white Chevy work pickup with the utility bed. On the ground next to the driver's side door, he spotted a man flat on his back. He was a big, strong man, about 6 feet tall, with a shaved head and tuft of beard on his chin. He wore an orange safety shirt, black tank undershirt, gray pants and black shoes.

Moncur could see that the man had a lump on his eye and blood around his mouth and right cheek. A large pool of blood congealed beneath his head and upper body. His right arm extended from his body as if hailing a cab. The body showed signs of lividity, the purple discoloration caused by blood pooling under gravity at low points in the body after the heart stops. Just behind the man, red spots were splattered on an open refrigerator door. A sign on the wall read: "A culture of commitment to safety to each other."

Moncur radioed for a paramedic and walked carefully out of the garage so as not to step on any evidence. He asked Alvarez to cordon off the area as a crime scene.

Within minutes, an ambulance and a paramedic truck raced into the complex. Two emergency medical technicians took the man's vital signs and ran a field EKG reading. No signs of life. The EMTs called a physician at the Kern Medical Center in Bakersfield, recited their findings.

At 7:06 p.m., the man was officially declared dead. Over the next half hour, phone calls went out to supervisors and investigators, plus crime scene technicians and the coroner. Moncur started a crime-scene log to keep track of what would be a small invasion of law enforcement personnel overnight.

He then waited an hour and a half.

Covering more than 8,000 square miles, Kern County is just smaller than the entire state of New Jersey. But with 880,000 people, it has only a tenth of its population. Kern County is vast and in most places, empty. The rectangular-shaped county is made up of sprawling farmland, rugged mountains and wide swaths of desert.

The closest detective was more than an hour's drive away in the county seat of Bakersfield. Randall Meyer of the robbery homicide division got the call at home from the Kern County Sheriff's Office Communication Center at about 7:30 p.m. A former patrol deputy, training supervisor and investigator in the sex crimes unit, Meyer had been transferred to robbery-homicide six months earlier. He put on a suit and tie and headed east for Tehachapi.

He got to the top of the pass at 8:30 p.m. Pulling off Highway 58, he made his way on side streets to Goodrick Drive to the industrial complex. He flashed his ID, got logged in and was directed to the crime scene through two checkpoints, one at the outer perimeter near the entrance to the facility, the second the taped-off inner perimeter closest to the garage.

Darkness had come to the high desert. At an elevation of more than 4,000 feet, even on this summer night the temperature would plunge more than 40 degrees to the mid-50s. The complex was ablaze with emergency lights and full of cops.

Meyer received a briefing from another Kern County detective, Mitchell Adams, who was in charge of processing the crime scene. Adams had phoned another detective with instructions to seek a search warrant from a night-duty judge. In the meantime, Adams had an evidence tech videotape the exterior of the garage. He walked around to the back of the building, looking for any signs of evidence. Behind the garage, in the hard-parked dirt, he spotted what looked like footprints near the back door. He had the tech photograph those. About 15 feet west of the corner while waking southeast, he found another shoe track, also photographed.

After 90 minutes, Adams had a search warrant and for the first time entered the garage. Adams told Meyer that he followed the same path as Shaun Ware along the right side of the truck, stepping over the glass shattered into a powder. The fixture above was missing one of its two fluorescent bulbs and Adams could see some damage to the metal frame.

On the ground, directly below the fixture, he spotted a bullet. It was mangled from apparently hitting the light fixture. It appeared to be a larger caliber, .44 or .45, from a big, powerful gun.

To his right, through the office door, he could see a television, sofa, desk and office chair, exercise machine, photocopy machine, whiteboard, calendar and two desks against the wall. The bottom desk drawers were open and items, including file folders, had been removed and thrown on the floor. Behind the bookcase on the northwest wall were several binders on the ground that Adams believed had been hastily removed from their previous location. Two cell phones sat on the desk.

Walking around the front of truck, Adams saw the body for the first time, the blood on the face and a bump on the back of the head. Behind the man, red dots from blood spatter were on the doors of the refrigerator.

An evidence technician photographed the interior of the office, the bullet fragment on the ground, the tiny blood spatter on the interior of the refrigerator door, the door of the truck—everything Adams pointed out.

That was the extent of the physical evidence. Beside the footprints, Adams found nothing that a killer or killers would have left behind. An evidence tech dusted for fingerprints, but analysis would take days.

"I immediately started thinking that it was possibly a staged scene," Adams later said in court, repeating what he told Meyer. "In numerous investigations, with burglary and robberies and such, I've never seen items placed as those were and the amount of items."

How the victim died would remain a question mark. The bullet on the ground and the blood on and around the body suggested he was shot. The bump on the head could have come from a blow. An autopsy would sort that out.

No gun or other weapon was found. Nor did they find spent brass ammunition shells, suggesting the shooter used a revolver or picked up the ejected shells from a semi-automatic.

Meyer was led to the "reporting party," Shaun Ware. A burly man with a shaved head, Shaun could have been the victim's brother. Shaun explained that the garage was leased by Burlington Northern Santa Fe Railway as a repair shop.

He and the victim, whom he identified, worked as "rapid responders," going into the field when trains break down, which they had a habit of doing on the Tehachapi Pass.

From the flat San Joaquin Valley, the trains strain up the grade, so steep in one spot that the tracks form a circle, like a spiral staircase, that takes the trains up 77 feet in a mile. Train buffs flock from around the world to see the famed Tehachapi Loop. YouTube is full of scenes of the loop.

Some 20 trains a day labor up the pass, making it one of the busiest stretches of single track in the country and one of the hardest on engines. Metal cracks, hoses blow, wires short circuit. That's when the phone rings in the BNSF garage in Tehachapi. A rapid responder jumps in a truck and races out to the scene of the breakdown, diagnosing the problem and making repairs.

Shaun told the detective the Tehachapi responders work 12-hour shifts. They always work alone. The 7 p.m. to 7 a.m. shift the night before belonged to Shaun, that day's 7 to 7 to Robert Limon.

The last time he'd spoken to Robert was that morning during the 7 a.m. shift change. They talked about Robert's iPad, which was not working. Shaun slept all day before his overnight shift and had no idea what Robert had done during the day shift.

Meyer asked Shaun how well he knew Robert. He said he'd worked with him off and on for about two years. "He was a very friendly guy, very outgoing," Shaun later said in court, repeating what he told Meyer.

Robert was married with two kids and lived in a community called Silver Lakes, in the town of Helendale, in San Bernardino County, about an hour-and-half drive away toward Barstow. Shaun had never known Robert to use drugs or have been involved in any illegal activities. He couldn't think of anybody who'd had an argument with Robert, much less want to harm him.

Then Shaun said something that Meyer found particularly intriguing. Robert did not usually work in Tehachapi. He was based far across the Mojave Desert to the east at Barstow Yard, BNSF's sprawling rail classification yard where rolling stock is changed between engines along a labyrinth of tracks. According to Shaun, Robert was filling in that Sunday for the regular responder, who was either out sick or taking vacation time. Shaun didn't know which employee was out but he knew that Robert had taken the shift at the last minute.

Shaun told him something else: the BNSF work truck in the garage, like all trucks, was equipped with a forward facing camera that activates during accidents. It may have captured something.

When the processing of the scene was complete, the body was released to the coroner's investigator, who put bags over the hands to preserve evidence and pulled the wallet from the victim's back pocket. The driver's license confirmed what Shaun Ware had said. The victim was Robert Limon, age 38, with a home address on Strawberry Lane in Helendale.

The coroner investigator and two other body removal assistants placed the corpse into a blue body bag and sealed it with a tag. Robert Limon—husband, father and railroad worker—was now coroner number C01615-14.

One of the cell phones in the office belonged to Robert. It had several missed phone calls and text messages. The last text came at 8:30 p.m.: "Babe I'm worried about you. Call me. Leanna wants to say goodnight."

Det. Randall Meyer would find out that the text had come from Robert's wife, now widow.

It was never returned.

http://wbp.bz/boda

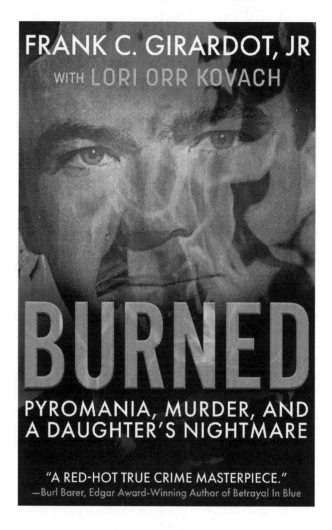

Chapter 1: Fire Season

Anyone who says there are no seasons in California hasn't been there.

In the Golden State, seasons are not things that rely on weather alone. The four seasons aren't necessarily tied to celestial movements or planetary alignment, either. Like a traffic jam on a Sunday morning that seems to have been caused by nothing, California seasons just happen and, like the freeways, seasons have names—just not spring, summer, winter or fall—like a quartet of hippie children.

Just as they know the difference between the San Diego, Santa Monica and Hollywood freeways, natives—and longtime residents of Southern California—know the difference between rainy season, hay fever season, June gloom and fire season.

The Southern California skyline—dominated by a mountain range alternately called the Santa Monicas, the San Gabriels or the San Bernardinos—holds the clues. Typically, those clues are the opposite of what one might think. When the air is cold and the Los Angeles or San Gabriel rivers thunder below their snow-capped sources carrying giant boulders and snapped tree trunks down steep mountainsides and into the vast cement canyons of the basin, it's rainy season.

No one knows how to drive in the rain. And most vehicles are not prepared for it. Think, for example, how day after day of 100-degree heat can affect skinny rubber wiper blades. It dries them out. And eventually when it rains, no one in L.A. who has a car that's more than two years old can see out the windshield. Think also about all that oil and dust that's collected on the freeway. It hasn't been washed away for months. None of this stops an Angelino from doing 80 miles per hour between destinations and inevitably getting in an accident because he or she couldn't see or couldn't stop fast enough on slick pavement. And that leads to hours and hours of extra time on the road for commuters.

In short, rainy season can shut down L.A. Too much water too fast and freeways simply flood. Sometimes, the mountains of dirt that create a barrier between the freeway and an adjoining neighborhood simply collapse in a slide that can shut down roads for days, if not weeks. And it's not just the freeways that are affected. Suburban neighborhood streets built atop flattened paths in the foothills before the advent of modern engineering can revert into ancient creeks moving mud-laden cascades along their way to ancient beaches that were formed over millions of years as the streams and arroyos of prehistoric L.A. carried their cargo of silt to the sea.

The docile brook that is the Los Angeles River and an urban canoe destination for hipsters can become a raging torrent that has been known to wipe out entire homeless encampments on its banks.

Rainy season is followed by hay fever season. In late winter and early spring, gray fields and brown hills become colorful impressionistic paintings. Green grass, orange California poppies, purple and blue lilacs and yellow wild mustard fill the skies with pollen and dust that produce epic amounts of allergies and wonderment.

Hay fever season usually lasts until the first heat wave—or at least until the jacarandas lose their flowers. Then spring is over.

At the end of spring, there's this weather pattern that some in L.A. call June gloom. It's the time of year when every day is a cliché. Some might say it's the movie "Groundhog Day" in real life. The beginning is usually marked by stories of black bears lounging in the swimming pools of foothills homes or rummaging through garbage cans in the early morning. Watch enough weather reporters on TV, you'll learn the phrase "coastal eddy" and you'll just get sick of its companion phrase, "night and morning low fog along the coast clearing in the afternoon when temperatures will reach the 70s." It's pretty much what you'll hear for week after week ad nauseum.

Then the unbearable, suffocating and oppressive heat kicks in. You'll know the change has arrived when every home in the neighborhood is shuttered and all you can hear at high noon in some suburbs is the whine of air-conditioner compressors doing their best to keep Angelinos comfortable.

Fire season typically announces itself with catastrophe. As the skies clear and daily temperatures rise, all of those flowers, grasses and weeds that were so magnificent around Easter have turned to dry tinder. At the entrance to the Angeles National Forest above the San Gabriel Valley, there's a dial that looks like it could be the spinner from "Wheel of Fortune." A ranger is responsible for letting visitors know the daily fire danger rating. Usually, the ranger will turn a dial on the wheel to one of the pie slices that range in color from green to bright red as a way of visually explaining what should be readily apparent to anyone with half a brain.

The fire danger slices are coded "low-moderate," "high," "very high," "severe," "extreme" and "catastrophic."

Even the bears, deer and mountain cats have a sense of the change in conditions; the weaker of the species will take great risks at the beginning of fire season. In a fire, the more seasoned predators such as bears and red-tailed hawks will hunt weaker prey seeking to escape the blaze. Other animals, including the cats, will hunker down in dens and wait it out.

To the public not traveling in the forest or encountering the wheel of misfortune, the National Weather Service will use local media and law enforcement bulletins to post red flag warnings and fire weather watches to "alert fire departments of the onset, or possible onset, of critical weather and dry conditions that could lead to rapid or dramatic increases in wildfire activity."

There is also a sliding scale for the severity of those of warnings. A red flag warning usually means that if a fire occurs in the foothills or mountains around L.A., the result will be extreme. One step below that is the fire weather watch, which means fire danger is high, but manageable.

Before any catastrophe, fire season has its signs—even if they are only present for a few hours, they are apparent: low humidity, strong winds and clear skies. During fire season, departments around California place additional firefighters on duty, staff more fire engines and keep equipment sharp and ready to roll.

Like anything and everything in Southern California, nothing really follows the rules. One day it's foggy and cool and the next, residents of a foothills community peppered with fancy real estate are fleeing a fast-moving and out-of-control brush fire.

Live in L.A. long enough and you'll understand it. But knowing when there's an advantageous change in the weather takes an expert: someone like a firefighter—or an experienced arsonist. Someone who watches for the change and can smell it in the air.

Glendale, a Los Angeles suburb nestled in the foothills between Pasadena—home of the famed annual Rose Bowl—and the San Fernando Valley found itself at the emergence of the 1990 fire season, the intersection of the dangerous weather pattern and an arsonist bent on destruction. The result—a catastrophe—was the $50 million College Hills Fire, which claimed 46 homes and damaged 20 others. There were injuries, but fortunately no one was killed.

While the foothills above L.A. burned, a predator lurked at the outskirts of Glendale, snapping photos and watching his prey flee.

The Pillowcase Pyro was in his element. He'd been doing this for years.

Chapter 2: Verlin Spencer

South Pasadena, Calif., could be Anytown, U.S.A. After all, the fabled Route 66, called the Mother Road by its admirers, cuts through its center just as it did (winding from Chicago to L.A.) through St. Louis, Oklahoma City, Amarillo, Gallup, Flagstaff, Kingman, Barstow and San Bernardino.

On the surface, South Pasadena is a town not all that different from Winslow, Ariz., or Galena, Kan., other spots on America's Main Street. There is a family-owned corner drugstore with a working soda fountain, parks, tree-lined streets and a public library that is open most days of the week.

A boutique grocery store still employs a staff of butchers and sells penny candy in bulk. The South Pasadena High School football team fills its stadium on Friday nights during football season and Homecoming Week is nearly a holiday.

South Pasadena residents are civic-minded. They care about their quality of life and working together, and were able to prevent the building of a massive freeway that would have sliced the tiny community of 30,000 residents in half. The construction would have completely changed the nature of a mostly unchanged suburb.

While South Pasadena shares a longstanding connection with its sister communities on Route 66, it also has something that makes it unique—it's just a few miles from the financial center of Los Angeles and less than a dozen miles from Hollywood. In fact, that proximity has made

South Pasadena a somewhat familiar backdrop in dozens of movies. South Pasadena's civic landmarks can be found in films as diverse as "Step Brothers" and "Halloween."

In spite of its gentle nature, the community hasn't always had it easy.

On May 6, 1940, South Pasadena was the site of one of the nation's first mass school shootings. The memory is only now fading, but the scars may never heal.

Tragedy happened because Verlin Spencer, the South Pasadena/San Marino Middle School principal, went on a shooting spree that morning. He said he couldn't control himself. Years later, he claimed he didn't even remember what happened. But there were some pretty good reporters back in the day who took notes.

So, when Spencer set out to kill those who had wronged him, he made good on the promise. By day's end, five were dead and one seriously injured. It wasn't like folks didn't see it coming. Spencer was somewhat of a crackpot and a very weird-looking dude. Thin-faced, Spencer kept his hair close-cropped on the sides, but maintained a wave on top that covered his receding hairline. He was also a potential molester who dosed himself daily with a combination of drugs including potassium bromide, which was used by doctors in the early half of the 20th century to suppress erections.

The genteel standards of journalism in 1940 didn't really allow reporters to reveal what Spencer's actual problems were. His proclivities were only hinted at. One can guess a doctor, acting on medical and pharmacological knowledge we would now consider barbaric, got Spencer to suppress his sexual impulses via chemical castration.

Apparently, the bromides and barbiturates also eliminated Spencer's sense of right and wrong. His plan to kill several co-workers at the school began early in the morning. Before leaving for work, Spencer dashed off a letter to his wife, telling her he had been fired from his job as principal and couldn't stand to live any longer. According to news accounts at the time, the note was also his will, which read: "I Verlin Spencer being of sound mind. This is my last will and testament and leave all my property to my wife Polly. This will become null and void if she spends more than $200 on my funeral expenses."

Spencer, 39, exhibited no outward signs of mental illness. Born in 1902, he had a normal childhood and graduated from a teacher's college in Colorado before entering Stanford and later, the University of Southern California.

In what would become a standard line in just about every news story on a mass shooting or serial killer in the 20th century, Spencer's hometown newspaper, the Greeley, Colo., Republican noted: "Former classmates of Spencer in Greeley were dumbfounded at the story of the tragedy in California. They described Spencer as a good student of the studious, non-athletic type of kindly, genial disposition and excellent reputation."

Anyway, on the morning of May 6, Spencer arrived in the school district's administration office and asked for a meeting with three co-workers. When the group was seated, Spencer pulled a pistol from his belt and began firing. Killed in the office were South Pasadena school Superintendent George Bush, 56; John Alman, 52; and Will Speer, 55. After shooting the men, Spencer got up, walked from the room, calmly closed the door and pointed his gun at Bush's receptionist, Dorothea Talbert. She thought the gunshots she heard were backfires from a student's car.

"He was leaning against the doorway. He said nothing to me at all. After he fired at me the first time, it seemed that he was waiting to see what the effect of it was," Talbert recalled. "He held the gun up close to his eyes. After he fired a second time, I fell."

Talbert survived, but two of Spencer's co-workers at the junior high were not as lucky. After driving the few blocks from the administration building to his school, Spencer got out of his car and tracked down teacher Venner Vanderlip, who was teaching the school's wood shop class. Spencer lured him from the classroom by saying he needed help with a student who had been hurt. Vanderlip followed Spencer into the hallway and was shot to death.

Before leaving the school grounds, Spencer encountered longtime art teacher Ruth Sturgeon, who was about to retire. He shot her once in the head. She slumped dead at her desk, where a note on her calendar read, "26 days to go."

Spencer then found his way back to his car, awaited the arrival of police and when they had him cornered, he held a shotgun to his chest and pulled the trigger.

Unfortunately, Spencer survived. He was sentenced to state prison and released in 1970 on a technicality after 30 years behind bars. He moved to Hawaii and was never heard from again.

South Pasadena's next tragedy would also be a mass murder. A mad man's killing of four innocents who died in a hardware store on a crisp fall evening nearly went unnoticed—much to the dismay of their killer.

http://wbp.bz/burneda

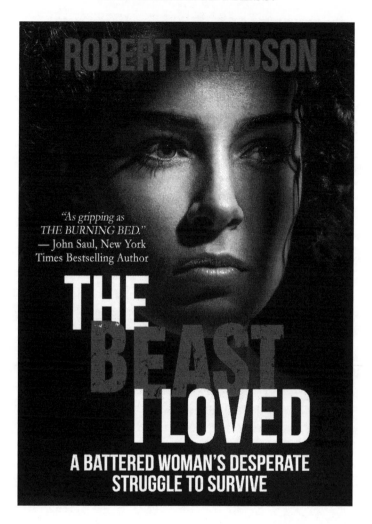

PART I: A BIZARRE & BRUTAL CHILDHOOD

No one went down to the cellar in the old farmhouse. For one thing, water rats the size of skunks lived there. And for another, "it was haunted." The damp, foreboding house, covered with weathered, brownish-black shingles, sat alone atop a knoll in a quiet old community in a remote part of Merrimack, New Hampshire, where neighbors were distant — both geographically and socially. Not one of them had come by to welcome the Jacksons to the neighborhood the day they moved into their new residence, and no one was there when they moved out three weeks later.

The neighborhood, located near the western bank of the Merrimack River in southern New Hampshire, was nothing like the town of Hudson, some ten miles further south, from which the Jacksons had moved near the end of 1968. There, the modest home they had occupied on B Street was located in an unremarkable middle-class neighborhood full of dogs, cats, and giddy children who played hopscotch on the sidewalk, and often stopped by the Jacksons to play pinball on one of the brightly-lit machines June's grandfather, Harold, had renovated and set up in the garage.

Merrimack, on the other hand, had anything but the carnival atmosphere of B Street. Though June wasn't sure of the "creepy sounds" coming from under the old pine floor boards each night, she knew the rats were real when one morning, while standing in the kitchen before going off to her kindergarten class, her grandmother suddenly gasped, turned even more ashen than she already was, and let loose with a primal scream emanating from deep in her tortured soul.

June's grandmother, Mary Jackson, was a fearful, deeply religious woman who seldom spoke, and when she did, often quoted scripture or other doomsday proclamations while thumping on her well-beaten Bible. Fifty-four and already completely grey-haired, Mary had shrunk into a four-foot-ten "plump butterball," but looked taller because of her erect posture and equally rigid demeanor.

Normally it took a great deal to shake the stoic woman, but she weakened when it came to such things as insects, snakes, rodents, and the like. Rats, after all, were "of the devil," the type of "signs" he would have sent to those whose thoughts were less than pure. And whose might fit such a category? Surely not Mary's. Nor June's nor her sister Diane. Perhaps Harold was thinking impure thoughts? He did spend an inordinate amount of time poking around in the musty netherworld of rats and whatever else dwelled in that godforsaken pit under the house. Pestilence, disease, famine — all of it, according to Mary Jackson, came directly from Satan himself.

Apparently heeding his call, water rats regularly made their way up the banks of the Merrimack and into the warm cellars of the older homes in the area. Having no contact with her neighbors, Mary Jackson had no way of knowing that it was not just she who suffered from such a plague — a plague made frightfully evident that morning when a duo of stealthy black varmints found their way up the cellar stairs and somehow squeezed their fat, wet bodies under the kitchen door.

Standing at the kitchen sink, Mary saw movement out of the corner of her eye, and instinctively turned to see, not three yards from her slippered feet, the devil's messengers scurry across the floor and disappear into the dark space behind the old Franklin stove. Mary Jackson had witnessed it all, and screamed to All Mighty God above for help. But the help came from a soft voice below.

"Grammy, do you want me to stay home with you?" asked five-year-old June, looking up at her anguished grandmother. Rather than acknowledge her granddaughter's offer of consolation (she rarely acknowledged that the child even existed), Mary turned on her heel and bolted for the living room where, as he did every morning, Harold Jackson sat reading the morning paper and watching the news on a television that was switched on at dawn and off at midnight most evenings.

Harold was a gaunt, serious man who looked well in excess of his sixty years. Other than his horn-rimmed glasses and salt-and-pepper mustache, his most noticeable features were his meshtopped fisherman's hat — which he rarely removed — and the cheap briar pipe he perpetually clamped between his brown-stained teeth. He occasionally puffed on a Sherlock Holmesstyle calabash pipe, and sometimes switched to his dime store corncob. But mostly he favored his cheap Dr. Grabow pipe, in which he smoked a sickeningly sweet mixture of Turkish tobacco and cherry syrup.

The fisherman's hat, however, was more wishful thinking than anything else. The one and only time he took his granddaughters fishing, he proved that he was, in fact, a fraud.

"He was scared out of his wits when we started rocking the boat. A dragonfly buzzed around us in the row boat and when we swiped at it, the boat rocked. When we got back to shore, Grandpa was shaking like a leaf. He told us later that he was scared to death because he couldn't swim. Then we found out that the big trout he used to bring home for supper were really from the hatchery where his friend worked. He let Grandpa net the breeders, but we always thought he caught them and that he was a great fisherman."

Like his wife, Harold had little to say to the grandchildren. This morning, however, he muttered a few words to June, who wasn't sure whether she should leave for school or stay home and somehow help her distressed grandmother.

"Run along, June," said Harold as he hobbled into the kitchen, still hunched over as if molded permanently by his beloved La-ZBoy recliner. He clutched his crumpled paper in one hand, and his black glasses rested crooked just above the swollen bulb of his veiny red nose. June knew not to question him, and on second thought, decided it was best to get out of the house before the hysterics began.

As for the other unexplained sounds coming from somewhere below the living quarters of the hundredyearold farmhouse, at least some of them had to be the handiwork of Bloody Bones and his partner Soap Sally. According to "weird Uncle Bill," they lived down in the dank cellar and would grab you the moment you reached the bottom of the cellar stairs. Uncle Bill related the story to then five-year-old June and eleven-year-old Diane one night as the rain relentlessly beat against the building's weathered shingles.

He explained that Bloody Bones would dismember you one limb at a time "so you got to see yourself gettin' ripped apart;" then he'd toss you over to Soap Sally who would grind you down and make soap out of you, and sell the bars off the back of her soap wagon to neighbors who would ask, "Pardon me, miss, but have you seen the little girls who live in that old farmhouse down the way? They seem to be missing."

"Yep, I seen 'em not too long ago," she'd say. "Think it was down in their cellar. Why not go down and take a look for yourself, heh, heh, heh?" And so, by this clever ruse, Soap Sally would keep herself and Bloody Bones in business forever and ever.

The teller of this tale was Bill Parker, a distant uncle whose roots were never determined, and who visited now and then from Alabama. As a house gift, he always brought with him a supply of his homemade, 150-proof moonshine, bottled and labeled in mason jars he stored in the trunk of his car.

During one visit, he had just walked around to the trunk and was twisting off the lid of one of the jars, about to give June and Diane a taste, when Mary caught sight of him and bellowed from the front porch, "Don't you *dare* give those girls that poison of yours, Bill Parker! Why, of all the crazy things I have ever seen!"

Mary was not, however, adverse to accepting a few jars for her own "rainy day," and settled down the moment Uncle Bill carried into the house a half dozen jars of the clear firewater he was so proud of.

Besides being a brew master, Uncle Bill was an avowed and openly proud member of the Birmingham chapter of the Ku Klux Klan, and often talked about the Klan meetings he attended. On one visit to the Jacksons, he told another story, this one true and bloodcurdling, and verified with photos from the homicide book he liked to carry around and show off, or just leaf through while sipping lemonade on the back porch.

A policeman for the city of Birmingham, Uncle Bill was not above boasting about how, a few months earlier, he and his "boys" burned out the Birmingham headquarters of the Black Panthers. This was the late 1960's, when the Black Panthers were at the height of their power and prestige, and with leaders such as articulate, rebellious young men like Huey Newton, Eldridge Cleaver, and Bobby Seale. Uncle Bill had no affection whatsoever for "that element," and went on to tell how, just before the burning, a lynching had occurred.

A young black man had been accused of some sort of indiscretion with a white woman — perhaps looking at her for a little too long — and for it was summarily hung by his neck from an old oak tree situated high on a hill that could be clearly seen from the town where he had lived. "They used that tree in particular," said Uncle Bill, "to teach the rest of them bloods a lesson."

While telling the story, Uncle Bill flipped through the homicide book, which contained photographs of numerous infamous killings. "Want to see what happens to uppity niggers?" he asked the girls. Not waiting for a response, he found the page he was looking for and thrust the book into June's lap, pointing contemptuously to the photo of the unfortunate young man hanging from the tree.

"It was terrible. The man had been hanging there for days and his neck had stretched out about three feet. It was so ugly to look at. I can't believe Uncle Bill showed it to us little kids. He said he was mad, and that blacks ... well, niggers was the word he used ... he said they were taking too many liberties with our white girls. He said, 'I wanted the bastard's head to come off but it just wouldn't. Damn, he was a stubborn nigger!'"

A week after the rat incident, a torrential storm raised the Merrimack River to within a foot of its banks and sent rats by the thousands scrambling for high ground — and warm cellars. Another rat incident — this time in the middle of dinner — along with a house full of pots and buckets filled to their brims with malodorous water from a badly-leaking roof, was enough to drive the Jacksons out of their new abode and into another house back in Hudson, New Hampshire.

Though they returned to their old town, the Jacksons selected a different area and now lived on Pinedale Avenue in a quiet neighborhood occupied mostly by older people without children. Their colorless ranch house at the end of a dead-end street rested atop a steep fifty-foot cliff, which fell off precipitously into a tributary of the Merrimack River.

Because of the treacherous dropoff, virtually no children lived at this end of the street. But Mary Jackson was delighted to be here, certain that the fifty vertical feet between her and the water would alleviate any further rodent problems. And Harold was content to settle into the nicest house he had ever rented.

In the past, Harold Jackson had made enough money to get by working as a security guard. Then he found work as a laborer in a paper factory where he doubled his income and was able to put away small amounts of money for his retirement. Now, at sixty, he was enjoying the "golden years," and spent the better part of his day plopped in his threadbare, green and orange plaid recliner. His wife had a similar model, but it was upholstered in "antique brown Naugahyde," which she adored.

Sitting side by side, Mary held her own, keeping up Harold's regimen of watching virtually every soap opera, game show, and news story available from dawn till dusk. This was 1968, before television remote controls were widely used, so for the most part, the Jacksons simply selected a channel, sat back, and took in all that it had to offer for hours on end.

It was, in part, because of these two beloved vices—the television and the recliners—that the Jacksons paid so little attention to their adopted granddaughters. One had to consider the fatigue factor as well: Having raised eight children of their own, the Jacksons had little interest in raising their daughter's castoffs.

June had been dumped at the front door of her grandparents' home the day she was born, as had her sister six years earlier. Their mother, Ann Jackson, was neither capable nor interested in raising children — she only enjoyed making them. Diane was sired by one man, June by another, and Dan, who came along three years later, by yet another unnamed and unknown father whom Ann had met and bedded after one of her nightly drinking bouts in an equally undistinguished local bar.

Diane was the product of a tryst between Ann and a married man who lived in a house behind the Jacksons'. Likewise, June was the result of another affair, only this time Ann knew her suitor much longer. She had been having sexual relations with the man for several months until his wife died in a freak accident one sunny Saturday afternoon in Hudson, New Hampshire. While watching a stock car race, a car suddenly spun out of control and careened off the retaining wall. It flipped and sent a tire flying into the crowd, hitting the young woman and killing her instantly. Ann continued her affair with the man and eventually became pregnant with his child. In a bizarre display of deference for the dead woman, Ann named the baby after her—the woman's name was June.

"A complete absence of love" was how June characterized her childhood. "And quiet. It was too quiet in our house. My grandparents never spoke. They just didn't care about us, couldn't be bothered. There was no interaction between us: no input, no punishment when we misbehaved, nothing. We never went anywhere or did anything: no beach, amusement park, picnics — none of the normal things families did. We even made our own breakfast when we were little.

"I remember climbing up on the stool in the morning to get the cereal down from the cupboard. And when I took a bath, I took it alone. I didn't have rubber duckies or anything like that to play with. My grandmother would leave me and come back thirty minutes later to see me shivering in the cold water."

Apparently, the mothering flaw was genetic, for on the rare occasions that Ann Jackson took the time to come visit her daughters at her mother's house, she treated them exactly as their grandmother did. When she'd drive up in one of her boyfriend's cars, the girls were ecstatic, at least at first. By the end of the visits, June was always in tears.

June's routine was always the same: kneel by her mother's chair and tug at her sleeve trying to get her attention, saying over and over, "Mama, Mama, I'm so glad you're here, I have so much to tell you." But Mama was never interested in her younger daughter, and always turned her attention to Diane.

"I think I spent most of my childhood trying to get my mother's attention. And I never quit. Any normal kid would have given up at some point, but considering the source, I wasn't what you would call normal. I kept hoping against hope that my mother — or my grandmother or grandfather or *somebody* — would love me. They never did."

No one knew where Ann Jackson lived or what she did, but one thing they knew was that she was an alcoholic. And she was not an attractive woman. Perhaps the two issues were related. "She didn't have a very pretty face. And she was uneducated. I don't know if she went to school or for how long. I remember hearing something about reform school or a juvenile detention center."

But she compensated. Ann attracted men by wearing cheap perfume and outlandish clothes: big hoop earrings, bright red lipstick, tight pants. She was only five-foot-four, but made herself taller with spiked heels and a beehive hairdo. And it worked. She always had boyfriends (all heavy drinkers like her), but none of them stayed around very long.

"There was always someone new in Mom's life, and she was always complaining about them and her relationships. When we were a little older, all she'd do was complain about how terrible things were for her, and never ask how we were doing."

It's not that Ann Jackson didn't pay attention to her children. She did. But she had to be sufficiently inebriated to accomplish the task. "I made Mom a little troll doll out of plaster of Paris once. It was the ugliest thing you ever saw, but I couldn't wait until she came over so I could give it to her. I had painted it all different colors, and they all ran together; it was so bad!

"When she finally came by, she had been drinking, as usual. I handed her the doll and she looked at it and said, 'Oh, honey, it's beautiful. It's the most beautiful thing in the whole world.' And then she started to cry. She cried and cried and cried."

On another occasion, Ann Jackson came to see her daughters and again she was drunk. "This time she came to take us away, take us back. She had been drinking and she got all sentimental. She always got emotional when she drank. Sometimes she got mean too. She did that day.

"Mom seemed all right when she came in, but then she got into a big fight with my Aunt Margaret, who lived across the street and had come over when she saw my mother pull up. Mom was pounding on the walls and ranting about wanting her baby — me — back. She was running around the house like a madman trying to find me. Diane grabbed me and put me in the clothes hamper and told me not to make a sound. It was a wicker hamper and I could sort of see through it. I remember seeing this crazy lady running right towards me and then past me, not realizing I was watching the whole thing."

Three years prior, Ann Jackson had been successful in absconding with the children. She had taken them for the afternoon, saying she would buy them lunch and take them to the park. It sounded odd to Mary because her daughter never took the girls *anywhere*, let alone the park. When she did not return by five o'clock, Mary knew exactly what had happened: Ann took off with the children and drove day and night to Tennessee, where she had been living with her current boyfriend in a filthy apartment, but one well-stocked with whiskey and cigarettes.

The abduction, however, was not motivated by sentiment, it was driven by *money*. Ann discovered that she would be eligible for state aid if she was an out-of-work mother with children to support. Such was the case for Harold and Mary Jackson as well, who had been collecting a nice stipend from the state of New Hampshire — and were not about to give it up easily.

So, at five the following morning, Harold and Mary got in their Chevrolet station wagon and drove the thousand miles up and over the Appalachian Mountains to the address in Mary's address book, from which she had sent Christmas cards the previous season. The next afternoon, they knocked on the door of what turned out to be a dilapidated tenement on the outskirts of town rather than the "nice little apartment in Memphis" their daughter had described.

On entering, the Jacksons could barely believe what they saw: Crumpled newspapers and crushed beer cans littered every corner of the apartment. Ashtrays overflowed onto the floor, and cigarette butts lay where they were ground into the carpet. Paper plates with encrusted food were piled on a kitchen card table, and another pile of plates towered in the kitchen sink. The smell of stale beer and cigarette smoke permeated the air, as did an overpowering stench of dog urine and cat feces which, combined, had turned the lime green shag carpet into a blotchy mass of matted, dung-colored hair.

June and Diane, then two and eight, were naked and unwashed, and their stringy hair had osmotically taken on the look of the soiled carpet on which they played. Due to finances, their mother had never purchased disposable diapers and instead used cloth diapers, all of which Mary Jackson discovered stinking in the broken-down washing machine in the rear of the apartment.

When the elder Jacksons had entered the apartment, Ann was putting June into a highchair to give her a lunch of Wonder Bread and grape jelly. As usual, the woman was drunk, and now became highly agitated because of the unannounced visit by her parents. Having just locked June into the chair, she turned to face her parents.

"Oh no, you don't!" she barked, knowing full well why her parents had come.

As her mother made a move toward June, Ann grabbed the child and tried to pull her out of the highchair. But she forgot that she had locked her in, and so she struggled without success. Screaming from the pressure on her tiny thighs, June further incensed her inebriated mother, who began wildly screeching at her parents, Diane, and her boyfriend, who lay stretched out on the couch, drunk and oblivious to the ruckus going on around him.

The Jacksons collected the foul-smelling diapers in a green garbage bag, stuffed the rest of the girls' belongings into another bag, and headed back to New Hampshire, stopping at the first filling station to wash the girls the best they could and buy them sodas and cookies.

June and Diane did not see their mother until a year later when she pulled up to the house directly across the street from theirs on Pinedale Avenue. Ann got out of her car carrying a bundle wrapped in a blue blanket and slipped inside the house belonging to Ann's sister, Margaret.

Margaret was in her early thirties, a few years younger than Ann, and had been desperately trying to have a child, but without success. Just as she was giving up hope that she would ever have a child of her own (she had determined that she was sterile), Ann had her third child, Dan, in Tennessee. Though she would have received a few dollars a month from the state, Ann decided it wasn't worth the effort it would take to raise a child and gladly turned him over to her delighted sister.

There was, however, one condition that Margaret insisted on, and she made her sister swear on the Bible to uphold it: Dan could never know who his real mother was. He was never to be told where he came from, and as far as he was concerned, his mother was Margaret and his aunt was Ann — not the other way around.

Dan could never know that the little girls directly across the street were his sisters, nor were they supposed to know he was their brother. But a foul up had occurred: Ann had absentmindedly failed to call ahead to her mother, as planned, to remind her to keep the children away from the window when she drove up with the baby. And that's exactly where they were when she dumped off her third unwanted child. Now they had to be in on the lie, and they, too, had to swear on Mary Jackson's old Bible that they would never reveal to their playmate who he actually was.

"This was the beginning of a life of lies. When Mom would occasionally come to visit us, Dan would ask, 'Who is that lady going into your house?' We'd have to lie and say it was a friend of Grandma's. His own mother! And no one could tell him.

"The significant thing for me was that I learned at an early age that even though things seemed wrong or somehow out of place, it would all be okay if we kept it a secret, if nobody knew. Keep things hidden, pretend they weren't happening. It was the perfect training for what happened to me after I married my abusive husband."

As luck would have it, Aunt Margaret was not sterile after all, and went on to have three more children of her own. This was a boon for June and her sister, because without the four kids across the street to play with, the neighborhood would have been very quiet indeed. Few children lived on the block, and Mary Jackson couldn't be bothered interacting with her grandchildren. But she made an exception on Sunday mornings when she took them to her "fire and brimstone" church in downtown Hudson.

"It was the only time Grandma paid any attention to us. She made us get dressed in our Easter dresses and patent leather shoes, and we had to be ready to walk out the door by seventhirty sharp. It was a fourhour ordeal, starting at eight and not ending until noon. We hated it. Everyone was yelling and moaning, singing hymns praising Jesus with their hands waving in the air. It was right out of the movies."

Harold Jackson paid even less attention to his grandchildren than his wife did, living mostly in his own television world or tinkering mindlessly with contraptions he'd assembled and disassembled in the garage. But at least he provided some comic relief when he let his dog, Mort, sit at the dinner table after supper.

Mort was a mediumsized poodle with large patches of hair gnawed off his rump. He was allergic to fleas, and was constantly biting at the itchy skin or licking his private parts for hours on end, which kept them inflamed and bleeding.

After supper, Harold would interrupt Mort's maintenance rituals and call him to his place at the table where he sat like one of the family and joyfully lapped up the last drops of Harold's creamed tea. It was the only time the old man showed any emotion, happy that his poor brute was enjoying a respite from the itching that tormented it so and which kept the animal endlessly dragging its hind end across the carpet, trying for relief that never came.

"On top of everything else, Mort was an epileptic. He fit in perfectly with our dysfunctional family. He'd have a seizure and Grandma would go running for the Bible saying the demons were killing the dog. Then Grandpa would push her out of the way and try to hold Mort still while he was convulsing. And we two little kids were watching all this craziness around us."

But Grandma wasn't watching the kids. Though June was only five, she often found her way down the treacherous fiftyfoot cliff abutting the back of the Pinedale property, and was allowed by her oblivious grandparents to play along the riverbank and in the storm drainpipe that jutted from the side of the cliff.

One day, while sailing leaves down the drain, June looked up to see that a group of boys had followed her down to the river. They waited until she made her way into the twenty-foot-long pipe, then quickly boarded up the ends with scrap lumber they were going to use to make a fort. Only June's high-pitched wailing resounding off the cement pipe walls convinced the boys that their fort-building days would be over for good if they did not let the little girl go.

With her face muddy from tears and dirt, June clawed her way back up the cliff and reported the incident to her grandparents. But the timing wasn't right. All Mary Jackson could do was hush the child up, telling her, "Not now, our show is on! Get in the bathroom and clean yourself up, you're a mess!"

http://wbp.bz/tbila

More True Crime You'll Love From WildBlue Press

RAW DEAL by Gil Valle

RAW DEAL: The Untold Story of the NYPD's "Cannibal Cop" is the memoir of Gil Valle, written with co-author Brian Whitney. It is part the controversial saga of a man who was imprisoned for "thought crimes," and a look into an online world of dark sexuality and violence that most people don't know exists, except maybe in their nightmares.

wbp.bz/rawdeal

BETRAYAL IN BLUE by Burl Barer & Frank C. Girardot Jr.

Adapted from Ken Eurell's shocking personal memoir, plus hundreds of hours of exclusive interviews with the major players, including former international drug lord, Adam Diaz, and Dori Eurell, revealing the truth behind what you won't see in the hit documentary THE SEVEN FIVE.

wbp.bz/bib

THE POLITICS OF MURDER by Margo Nash

"A chilling story about corruption, political power and a stacked judicial system in Massachusetts."–John Ferak, bestselling author of FAILURE OF JUSTICE.

wbp.bz/pom

FAILURE OF JUSTICE by John Ferak

If the dubious efforts of law enforcement that led to the case behind MAKING A MURDERER made you cringe, your skin will crawl at the injustice portrayed in FAILURE OF JUSTICE: A Brutal Murder, An Obsessed Cop, Six Wrongful Convictions. Award-winning journalist and bestselling author John Ferak pursued the story of the Beatrice 6 who were wrongfully accused of the brutal, ritualistic rape and murder of an elderly widow in Beatrice, Nebraska, and then railroaded by law enforcement into prison for a crime they did not commit.

wbp.bz/foj

38351138R00130

Made in the USA
Middletown, DE
07 March 2019